George Huntston Williams
Christian Attitudes Toward Nature

WIPF & STOCK · Eugene, Oregon

Wipf and Stock Publishers
199 W 8th Ave, Suite 3
Eugene, OR 97401

Christian Attitudes Towards Nature
By Williams, George H.
Copyright©1970 by Williams, George H.
ISBN 13: 948-1-4982-2457-4
Publication date 10/15/2015
Previously published by Christian Scholar's Review, 1970

Introduction

GEORGE HUNTSTON WILLIAMS's (GHW) *Wilderness and Paradise in Christian Thought* (1962) remains a classic expression of Christian reverence for Creator, creation and enlightened human vocation. Less known is his subsequent survey, "Christian Attitudes Towards Nature," which appeared as a two-part essay in *Christian Scholar's Review* (1971-72). Williams' distinguished career as a Harvard church historian (1947-80) inspired two festschrifts: *Continuity and Discontinuity in Church History* (1979) at his 65th birthday and retirement from classroom teaching and *The Contentious Triangle: Church, State and University* (1999) at his 85th birthday on the eve of a new millennium. A selection from each volume serves to introduce George Williams' two foremost reflections on Nature.

Williams' student Timothy George, in his 1999 essay "A Historian for All Seasons," noted GHW's lifelong interest (both personal and scholarly) in "creation care." As a self-identified "Christian naturalist," GHW wrote to encourage "other writers to re-conceive the urgent problem of conserving wilderness areas and of extending wildlife refuges all over the world for perpetuation of endangered species" (ix). As Dr. George observes, "Fully cognizant that elements within the Judaeo-Christian tradition have been called upon to sanction the exploitation of nature, he finds ample resources within that same tradition for rethinking the ecological unity of humankind with the cosmos, for the elaboration of an "earth ethic," for a vision of the human as steward rather than manipulator of creation, as carers for our fellow creatures…rather than conquerors of the cosmos."

Williams' teacher (and later Harvard Divinity School colleague) James Luther Adams, in his 1979 essay "George Huntston Williams: A Portrait," offers further insight. "In his elaborate history of attitudes toward nature in Western history (1971), he traces the antimonies suggested by seven sets of scriptural passages. The great achievement of the covenantal religion of Israel was to disengage itself from the cults of fertility of the Caananites and to think of man as in this sense overcoming nature… Williams has not been willing to put to one side the theological concern for the cosmos, and for the earth and its diversified world in which all creatures have a precious place in God's eyes. There is grace from below as well as grace from above."

In this earlier *fest* another iconic church historian, Jaroslav Pelikan, praised his friend's range of thought in "Hundred-handed, Argus-eyed: The Historical Scholarship of George H. Williams." There, he cited the succinct assessment of Williams' valuing of nature by Yale president A. Bartlett Giamatti in *The Earthly Paradise and the Renaissance Epic* (1966): "brilliant discussion."

George Williams' heart for Nature, as he observed during my days as Harvard doctoral student and minister, was rooted in childhood experiences in rural Ohio, the witness of Scripture and subsequent studies in both history and the sciences. His appreciation of Harvard Divinity School (which he chronicled and helped rescue as Acting Dean in the 1950s), was deepened by that school's historic "errand into the wilderness." As Lynn White, Jr's 1967 *Science* essay "Historical Roots of the Ecological Crisis" inspired a swell of critical examination re Christianity and the impact of theology on environmental domination, so George Huntston Williams' works here provide both a redemptive voice from that era and continued resources for ecotheology (see bibliography) and creation care across generations. As he was fond of saying, we are "creatures of a Creator and subjects of a Kingdom."

James D. Smith III
The Feast of St. Francis of Assisi
Centennial of George Williams' birth
October, 2014

Rev. James D. Smith III (Th.D., Harvard) is professor of church history at Bethel Seminary San Diego and associate pastor of La Jolla Christian Fellowship.

In this essay the author, George Huntston Williams, explores the views of nature which have been held through the history of the Christian church. Professor Williams teaches at Harvard Divinity School. The essay will be concluded in the next issue of the Christian Scholar's Review.

Christian Attitudes Toward Nature

INTEREST in the domain of nature is well documented through the two thousand years of Christian history into our quite secularized age. The importance of examining historically the changing Christian attitudes toward nature is readily apparent in our day as we do battle against the continued pollution of earth, air, and water in an effort to establish new norms for the enhancement of the environment of man and for his stewardship of the myriad forms of life about him.

In this ecological interest, most authors and agents concerned to save what remains of the wilderness, to protect threatened wildlife and endangered species around the world, to resist the bulldozing and asphalting of America the once beautiful, all in chorus declare that the Bible, that Christianity, that Christian man-centeredness are largely responsible for the rape of nature in Christian/Western/technological civilization. Christianity is being, but quite mistakenly, characterized as a religion essentially opposed to nature, and is being held accountable directly or indirectly for the present ecological crisis in Western civilization. Christianity has fostered, critics have remarked, a doctrine of an original or all-pervasive sin; it has been suspicious of both flesh and reason; it has been preoccupied with the vagaries of sex. It took organized form in the cities of the Graeco-Roman world rather than in the countryside (of the *pagani*); and, though some of its most zealous devotees later fled to the desert, it in general fled the world of human affairs, only to opt primarily for political rather than pastoral metaphors and nature imagery, all because of the Church's dread of the cults of fertility and power and associated idolatry. Before Christians, Hebrews in the prophetic line of Elijah, devoted to the Lord God of hosts (of battle), were fearful of the cultus of the *baalim;* and, though they vindicated Yahweh as Lord not only of history but also of creation, they did this only by remaining congenitally uneasy about his becoming too much involved in rain, fertility, and harvests. Judaism and Christianity, their detractors argue, have alike contributed through the Bible the ideology of the exploitation of nature.[1] Historically, the Christian attitudes towards nature and human nature, ever reworking the texts of the Old and the New Testament, have been more complex than the foregoing characterization of Christianity as suspicious of, hostile toward, or exploitative of and utilitarian toward nature. It will be the purpose of this paper to bring into relief several recurrent antinomies in the Christian view of nature documented in two thousand years of Christian history. In getting at these basic attitudes in the Christian tradition, we also understand attitudes towards nature in Western civilization in general, because, of course, scriptural and Christian residues can live on quite persistently in secular or secularized forms. The half-life of a complex Christian compound is at least a century!

The writer, in presenting a very complex history under the heading of Christian attitudes towards *nature,* selects the latter term because this word, in Latin *natura* and in Greek *physis,* supplies us with the most comprehensive and accessible term for what we all have in mind in the present ecological crisis. To say *creation* is to prejudge the discussion theologically for fellow ecologists outside the Christian community of faith. To say *environment* is to be too man-centered. To say *world, cosmos, universe, matter, things* is to put the stress on the inorganic. To say *science* would be doubly misleading, for it would suggest a rehearsal of the perennial conflict between science and religion, reason and revelation, and would accent successive ways of seeking to know the world rather than, what is here intended, namely, to ascertain successive or simultaneous Christian attitudes towards, and assumptions about, nature. The term *natura/physis* has the further advantage of referring to what is both in man and about him. Thus what we are attempting to clarify are the different attitudes toward that which has been abidingly the concern of the physician, the physicist, and the metaphysician, the naturalist, the natural theologian, the natural lawyer, the natural historian, and the nature lover.

Now to bring all this within the range of one paper and to discern some pattern in so comprehensive a coverage of time and space and cultural permutation, one must be highly selective. The approach which follows is not that of a rough sketch of Christian attitudes towards nature, but rather that of a selection of some seven sets of scriptural texts, which have in fact bulked large in the Western cultural commentary, as it were, on nature, inspected through the lens of Scripture. These seven sets of scriptural texts have little to do with Aristotle's distinction of seven meanings of nature. Aristotle systematically defined nature,

---

1 An oft-cited and influential presentation of this point of view is that of Lynn White, son of a Presbyterian manse, in *Machina ex Deo: Essays in the Dynamism of Western Culture* (Los Angeles, 1968). Professor Richard Wright of Gordon College dealt with the criticism of Lynn White and several others cited in his "Responsibility for the Ecological Crisis" in the first issue of *Christian Scholar's Review,* pp. 35-40.

first in his *Physics,* giving four meanings; but then, in his *Metaphysics,* further refining his distinctions, he gave us seven.[2] Nor do we have in mind the some seven good reasons which come to mind as to why Christians must always be more positive than negative toward the world order, toward matter and the flesh. For good measure, however, we should, perhaps, have these reasons before us first.

For at least seven reasons Christian theologians have been drawn to deal not only with creation, creatureliness, and contingency in a general way but also specifically, persistently, and systematically with matter, nature, flesh, and the creaturely world of innumerable species and kinds largely in a positive sense: 1) because their Scriptures revealed God as the Creator and the heavens and earth and all living things as his creation; 2) because Jesus Christ came to be understood as a Person in two natures (fully divine and fully human); 3) because that human nature in the doctrine of the Incarnation came to be understood as impersonated by the Logos, the Word of God or the Wisdom of God, in Proverbs and elsewhere regarded as the very instrument and author of the creation of all things; 4) because in baptismal theology the reborn in Christ was believed to acquire a *new nature* and thereby to participate in the *new creation* in the Holy Spirit; 5) because in one major (Catholic) development in eucharistic theology the very body of the God-Man, Creator and Redeemer, was held to materialize on the Christian altar; 6) because in their ethical theories Christians took seriously the institution of matrimony with the injunction to be fruitful and multiply even when holding aloft the ideal of vocational virginity and celibacy and they also took seriously the Christianization of society and the state and all its legitimate functions on the basis of natural law; and finally 7) because in Christian eschatology there has been place not only for the immortality of the soul but also for the resurrection of the flesh and a place also in the inauguration of the Kingdom of God for the purification of all creation to be redeemed for a new heaven and for a new earth.

Thus Christianity has not been an otherworldly religion indifferent to man's earthly environment and well being; but its theism has admittedly been anthropocentric rather than biocentric despite its comprehensive cosmogony. One might have expected, indeed, the scriptural stress on God as Creator in Judaism and Islam as well as in Christianity to have given an even greater prominence to all aspects of the created order — in contrast, say, to Hinduism, Buddhism, Taoism, Confucianism, or Shinto.

Largely in agreement with Professor Wright[3] in "Responsibility to the Eco-

---

[2] Aristotle, *Physics,* II, 1, 192; V, 8, 193b, p. 18; *Metaphysics,* V. 1014 b 16-1015 a 19. For a useful summary of recent literature on nature in Greek philosophy, see Robert Grant, *Miracle and Natural Law in Greco-Roman and Early Christian Thought* (Amsterdam, 1952), ch. 1.

[3] Above, n. 1. See further D. S. Wallace-Hadrill, *The Greek Patristic View of Nature* (Manchester/New York, 1968).

logical Crisis," that factors other than explicit theology are probably much more important in ascertaining basic human attitudes towards nature in whatever the religious culture, the present writer still feels that it is very much worthwhile to search the past to find how our Christian forebears made use of the same Scripture that guides us in finding solutions or suggesting strategies over the centuries of their dealing with nature. We turn now to the seven sets of scriptural texts that seem to have been unusually prominent in this ongoing Christian discussion from the close of the New Testament canon well into the nineteenth century.

SEVEN SETS OF SCRIPTURAL TEXTS ILLUMINATED IN HISTORY FROM CHRISTIAN ANTIQUITY INTO THE NINETEENTH CENTURY[4]

Distinct from the foregoing seven points at which Christian dogma and moral theology have taken nature seriously, especially human nature and the human condition, there are some seven sets of contrasting attitudes towards nature beyond our bodies and human needs. At this juncture it is possible to distinguish seven recurrent antinomies in the Christian attitude toward and understanding of nature, alike the internal human nature, the human condition, and the natural world in which humanity is shaped. It is incumbent on Christians who share the concerns of the more secular ecologists to seek to clarify for themselves the ways in which their spiritual forebears applied scriptural injunctions and metaphors for the relation of fallen and redeemed men to the natural order. And it is quite possible that their more secular colleagues in ecology will be likewise instructed.

The capital texts in Scriptures on creation, man, and nature, are of course concentrated in the cosmogony of Genesis. But there are many others. We shall be showing how the ideas of our Christian forebears in different ages and traditions have been formed by certain texts or, possibly, having been formed otherwise, found in the Scriptures a variety of sanctions for their views of nature.

There are three general points that should be made initially about the creation texts in Genesis (1-2) and the text on the fall of man of Genesis 3.

The patristic, scholastic, and later theological tracts and commentaries on Genesis, in particular on the six days of creation, constitute the most continuous body of Christian comment on nature. As a special genre of what might be called

---

[4] The author has these seven sets in brief in "The Background in Scripture and Tradition for Reassessment of a Christian Role in Wildlife Conservation and the Stewardship of Natural Resources," *Colloquy*, III, No. 4 (April, 1970), pp. 12-15. The author has dealt quite fully in book form with one or two of these sets in *Wilderness and Paradise in Christian Thought: The Biblical Experience of the Desert* (New York, 1962), esp. Part I, The Wilderness Theme, pp. 1-137. On the hexaemeron, see Frank E. Robbins, *The Hexaemeral Literure* (Chicago, 1912).

Christian cosmogony it is known as a hexaémeron: "hexaemeral (hexaemeric) literature" (from *hex* =6; *hēmera* = day).

With the earliest Jewish and Christian commentaries it was recognized as a problem to harmonize in God's holy Word what Old Testament scholars today identify as the majestic Priestly account of Genesis 1:1-2:4a and the simpler Yahwistic account of Genesis 2:4b - 2:24 (to the creation of Eve; ch. 3 the fall). The Yahwistic account is concrete and more anthropomorphic than the Priestly account and subordinates the cosmogonic features. Some commentators like the Jew Philo of Alexandria and Origen of Alexandria and Caesarea interpreted the Priestly strand as an account of the ideal man, possibly even before his embodiment in flesh, "the tunics" or "aprons" of Genesis 3:7. Platonic and Neoplatonic idealism would keep this interpretation alive into the Reformation Era.

The Priestly and the Yahwistic accounts in Genesis are alike anthropocentric. But there is room for varying combinations of emphases as between man's exploitive dominion and his benign stewardship of creation with also varying perceptions of the degree to which man was bound for his own good to respect the orders of creation.

It is to the whole range of use of the hexaemeral, prophetic, and other texts in both the Old and New Testaments *as they were used in the course of Christian history* that we now turn. The reader is again alerted to the fact that in clarifying the sets of seeming antinomies in Scripture the writer, as primarily Church historian, is dealing with these texts in their postbiblical context and only incidentally against their original Palestinian background.

I. THE INVOLVEMENT OR NON-INVOLVEMENT OF NATURE IN THE FALL OF MAN

The first set of scriptural antinomies is as follows: All of nature or creation is implicated in the fall of man. *Sed contra:* Alone man and the angels, because of their misuse of free will, are fallen; while nature flourishes unimpaired.

The Old Testament *locus classicus* for the involvement of nature with man is God's curse of Adam in Genesis 3:17c: "Cursed is the earth/ground because of you in your work." The New Testament confirmation of this is Romans 8:19; 22f.: "For the creation waits with eager longing for the revealing of the sons of God. . . .We know that the whole creation has been groaning in travail together . . . as we wait for adoption as sons, the redemption of our bodies."

The scriptural sanction for the less pessimistic view is Genesis 1:31: "And God saw everything that he had made, and behold, it was very good," but this was of course the divine assessment *before* the defection of Adam, and the text has remained in Christian history therefore inconclusive with respect to nature as it is. Hence, a stronger scriptural sanction in Christian history for the abiding goodness of creation and the non-involvement of nature in Adam's fall was

Psalm 19:1: "The heavens declare the glory of God; and firmament showeth his handiwork." Similarly Psalm 98:7f.:

> Let the sea roar, and all that fills it;
> the world and those who dwell in it.
> Let the floods clap their hands;
> let the hills sing for joy together.

Characteristic of the affirmative mood concerning nature as the handiwork of the Creator is the declaration of Clement of Rome (d. c. 96), leader of the very community to which Paul not much before addressed his Epistle with its pessimistic view of nature (Romans 8). In his Epistle to the Corinthians Clement, contemporary with several of the later writers of the New Testament, felt the benignity and harmony of nature as the living handiwork of God and his Logos:

> The heavens, revolving under His government, are subject to Him in peace. Day and night run the course appointed by Him, in no wise hindering each other. The sun and moon, with the companies of the stars, roll on in harmony according to His command, within their prescribed limits, and without any deviation. The fruitful earth, according to His will, brings forth food in abundance, at the proper seasons, for man and beast and all the living beings upon it, never hesitating, nor changing any of the ordinances which He has fixed. The unsearchable places of abysses, and the indescribable arrangements of the lower world, are restrained by the same laws. The vast unmeasurable sea, gathered together by His working into various basins, never passes beyond the bounds placed around it, but does as He has commanded. For He said, "Thus far shalt thou come, and thy waves shall be broken within thee." The ocean, impassable to man, and the worlds beyond it, are regulated by the same enactments of the Lord. The seasons of spring, summer, autumn, and winter, peacefully give place to one another. The winds in their several quarters fulfill, at the proper time, their service without hindrance. The ever-flowing fountains, formed both for enjoyment and health, furnish without fail their breasts for the life of men. The very smallest of living beings meet together in peace and concord. All these the great Creator and Lord of all has appointed to exist in peace and harmony; while He does good to all, but most abundantly to us who have fled for refuge to His compassions through Jesus Christ our Lord, to whom be glory and majesty for ever and ever.[5]

This blend of Stoic and Scriptural feeling for the created order, so beautifully expressed by the bishop of Rome in his mild rebuke of the Corinthians, must be read alongside other early Christian passages, in which nature was felt to be perverted. The comprehensive Pauline pessimism about the natural order, as groaning in travail with fallen man, commonly served as the lens for the Christian reading of even the notably optimistic view of nature in at least one strand in Hebrew Scripture. Over against these still orthodox views of the created order as created by God but fallen were the extravagantly pessimistic views of the Gnostic Christians of various sects and persuasions, who denied that the Creator of the visible universe, the Demiurge, was the highest God. In

---

[5] Epistle to the Corinthians, ch. xxvi.

monstrous webs of theosphy they spun out a view of the phenomenal world as something to be either shunned or programmatically abused, as they sought to disentangle themselves from matter, flesh, and the whole visible order of creation to return by *gnosis* and its various intellectual and cultic disciplines to the plenitude of divine fullness (Pleroma). Anti-creationist views were so strong on the margin of orthodox/catholic Christianity, especially in the second century, that for centuries to come there would remain the contagion of revulsion to the cosmos even in main-line Christianity, particularly within the ascetic movement. Orthodox/catholic Christianity was, however, content with a doctrine of original sin pervading mankind or creation at large, while Gnosticism and its sequels, like medieval Catharism, wholly repudiated the created world not only as fallen but even as the work of an inferior deity.

Whereas Judaism with the same scriptures bearing on the fall of man (Genesis) continued to be basically optimistic about the created order, Christianity, in competition with a variety of world-denying sects, of which Gnosticism was only the most hazardous because it claimed to be Christian, often developed rather somber views about nature.

The curse of mankind in Adam and Eve Christian Fathers found extended to nature as a whole, reinforced in the curse from the ground on Cain and in that on the whole wicked generation contemporary with Noah. The cumulative curse (Genesis 4:11f.) was in Christian tradition variously interpreted, however, as limited—to use the Vulgate—to the *humus* or as extended to the whole *terra;* and sometimes in Christian history a distinction would be made between earth and sea. The waters, at least, according to many were not affected by the curse and had come into their own in the Christian sacrament of baptism for purification from original sin.

A further post-biblical and clearly non-biblical complication of the original Hebraic cosmogony for patristic Christians was theological speculation about the possible corruption of nature with mankind in terms of the extra-biblical cosmic or mundane egg. We find this supplementary theory, for example, in the *Hexaemeron* of Basil the Great of Caesarea (d. 379). In commenting on (the Septuagintal) Genesis 1:2, he wrote:

How then did the Spirit of God move upon the waters? The explanation that I am about to give you is not an original one, but that of a Syrian [Ephraim Syrus]....He said ... that the Syriac word for *move* or *hover* was more expressive than the Greek, and that being more analogous to the Hebrew term it was a nearer approach to the scriptural sense. This is the meaning of the word; by "was borne" the Syrians, he says, understand: it cherished the nature of the waters as one sees a bird cover the eggs with her body and impart to them vital force from her own warmth.[5a]

[5a] *The Hexaemeron*, Homily II; *Nicene and Post-Nicene Fathers*, VIII, p. 63. As the survey being here presented is not a definitive monograph, the author is content to cite the readily available English translations of all texts, when they prove available.

In the beginning the Holy Spirit brooded over the aboriginal deeps as on a Mundane Egg, warming it and inducing differentiation as yolk, albumen, and shell. Christians in the patristic tradition of Basil speculated on the relationship of the original world called by God "good" to the present earth as reshaped by the Deluge, from which the second father of the race, Noah, was saved.

Well into the eighteenth century there have been two Christian interpretations with reference to this spherical egg of earth and "disfigurements" or "beautifications" in the form of mountains and plains. According to the negative interpretation reinforced by classical philosophical ideas about the perfection of the cosmic spheres beyond the earth (regarded in some cases as ensouled angelic beings), the earth was *originally* round, without high mountains or deep seas, and Paradise was in effect the whole of earth with but shallow, peaceful, and sweet waters. The present earth with deep oceans, high mountains, deserts, tundras, and jagged islands was, accordingly, thought of as a consequence of human sin: the bumps, warts, wens, and excrescences of the once perfect globe disfigured by man. According to the other interpretation, the present earth was regarded as essentially the same as that which left the hand of the Creator at the end of the sixth day—with or without modification of the theory of the Mundane Egg and the perfect spheres of outer space.

When our Christian forebears reflected on, viewed, or climbed a mountain, it made considerable difference whether in their theological cosmogony that mountain was regarded as a sign of perpetuated original sin or as an emblem of God's abiding goodness amid human sinfulness and weakness![6]

A representative early Christian exponent of pessimism about the whole of nature was the late second-century bishop of Antioch, Theophilus, who in his *Apology* to the pagan Autolycus argued as follows:

And on the sixth day, God having made the quadrupeds, and wild beasts, and the land reptiles, pronounced *no blessing upon them*, reserving his blessing for man, whom he was about to create on the sixth day.[7]

Then, after a diversion in which Theophilus also allegorized the quadrupeds as types of men who look not upward to their Creator and the birds as types of men who soar worshipfully toward God, he returned to real animals and made his point:

And the animals are named wild beasts (*theria*) from their being hunted (*thereusesthai*), not as if they had been made evil or venomous from the first — for nothing was made evil by

---

[6] Marjorie Hope Nicolson has traced the two traditions with special reference to the English literature of the seventeenth century in *Mountain Gloom and Mountain Glory: The Development of the Aesthetics of the Infinite* (Ithaca, N.Y., 1959).

[7] Theophilus, *Ad Autolycum*, ii, p. 17; *Ante-Nicene Fathers*, III, p. 101.

God, but all things good, yea, very good, – but the sin in which man was concerned brought evil upon them. *For when man transgressed, they also transgressed with him.*[8]

A later preacher and teacher in Antioch and then bishop of Constantinople, John Chrysostom (d. 407), commenting directly on the pessimistic Pauline chapter in Romans, asked rhetorically in a sermon for what cause and on what account all creation was groaning as in travail, and answered predictably: "On account of thee, O man. For since thou hast taken a body mortal and liable to suffering, the earth too hath received a curse, and brought forth thorns and thistles."[9] Here Chrysostom not inappropriately combined the negative natural theology of Genesis 3 and Romans 8.

It should be noted at this juncture that in saying that it was the earth that received the curse for Adam's sin, Chrysostom was opting for the more pessimistic sense of the passage. He had, in fact, a choice between what was undoubtedly intended in Genesis 3:17, namely, the soil, and the earth in the sense of the world. Moreover, Chrysostom construed the whole earth as suffering the curse to make fallen man's labor of the soil difficult. Chrysostom in saying "world" instead of "soil" was following the Septuagint.

In the Latin West the translation of the passage by Jerome (d. 420) was decisive: "Cursed is *terra* in thy work." Jerome thus connected the curse of the earth with fallen man's labor. If he had said, as he could have, in greater faithfulness to the Hebrew, "for thy sake," he would have even more fully intertwined fallen man's sin and the curse of the earth for generations of exegetes and preachers in Western Christendom to reflect upon.

Although Augustine of Hippo (d. 430) followed Jerome's line in accepting *terra* for the originally intended *humus*, he in fact interpreted the passage in that more limited sense of soil.[10] Augustine felt that nature only appeared to fallen man as unattractive. Actually it had remained largely untouched by his waywardness. To be sure, Augustine characteristically would not wish to have his parishioners love the world rather than its Creator, but in one sermon, for example, he asks rhetorically, with an unexpectedly sensitive perception of the goodness of creation apart from man:

But what is this evil world? For the sky and the earth and the waters and the things that are in them, the fishes and the birds and the trees are not evil. All these are good; it is evil men who make this evil world.[11]

---

[8] *Ibid.*

[9] John Chrysostom, Homily XIV in Romans 8:19f.; *NPNF*, XI, p. 444.

[10] *De Genesi contra Manichaeos*, xx; Migne, XXXIV, 211f.; *De Genesi ad litteram*, xxxviii; Migne XXXIV, 450; noted by Nicolson, *op cit.*, p. 85, n.21.

[11] Augustine, "Sermones ad Populum," 1st ser., 80, 9, *Oeuvres Complètes* de St. Augustin, XII, p. 273; quoted in Glacken, *Traces on the Rhodian Shore* (Berkeley, 1967), p. 197. See further Sister Mary Jane Holman, *Nature-Imagery in the Works of St. Augustine* (Washington, 1932).

Augustine in the *City of God* stated his view of the independence of nature from man even more beautifully:

And now, to pass from man to the rest of creation, what beauty for contemplation and what bounties for use God has scattered like largesse for man amid the weariness and miseries of this fallen and penalized lot! What words can describe the myriad beauties of land and sea and sky? Just think of the illimitable abundance and the marvelous loveliness of light, or of the beauty of the sun and moon and stars, of shadowy glades in the woods and of the colors and perfume of flowers, of the songs and plumage of so many varieties of birds, of the innumerable animals of every species that amaze us most when they are smallest in size. For example, the activity of ants and bees seems more stupendous than the sheer immensity of whales. Or take a look at the grandiose spectacle of the open sea, clothing and reclothing itself in dresses of changing shades of green and purple and blue. And what a delight when the ocean breaks into storm and can be enjoyed — at least from the shore where there is no fear of the fury of the waves![12]

In the Reformation Era Augustine's view of nature as not being implicated in man's sin was expressed by John Calvin (d. 1564), while the more pessimistic view of Chrysostom was expressed by Martin Luther (d. 1547). Standing in one line of tradition, Luther thought of the cosmos as the Mundane Egg, brooded over by the Holy Spirit. In his *Commentary on Genesis,* 1:2, he wrote: "And as a hen sits upon her eggs that she may hatch her young, thus warming her eggs and as it were infusing them into animation, so the Scriptures say the Holy Ghost brooded."[13] He thought of the original creation as a global paradise that was park-like, covering the better part of the earth without high mountains or unprofitable terrain like desert and tundra. He thought of the originally beautiful garden earth, only partly affected by Adam's and Cain's sinfulness, as lasting until the Deluge. Luther, a careful exegete, found Jerome's interpretation of the curse of the whole earth because of Adam more than the original Hebrew of Genesis 3:17[14] warranted; but then he went on to demonstrate from Scripture mankind's ongoing sin and God's enlargement of the curse upon nature, citing the sin of Cain whose brother's blood from the ground cursed him (Genesis 4:11f.) until at length God cursed the whole earth in the Deluge because of human sin (esp. Genesis 5:7, 11; 8:21). Craggy and sterile mountains and desert wastes were for Luther the direct consequence of the universal human sin and the avenging Deluge. Some of the features of the post-diluvian world, which were later to be regarded as natural beauties, for example, the mountains, Luther regarded as signs of sin:

As therefore since the Flood mountains exist where fields and fruitful plains before flourished, so there can be no doubt that fountains and sources of rivers are now found

12 *City of God;* tr. by Walsh *et al.* (N.Y., 1958), p. 529.

13 Commentary on Genesis 1:2.

14 Luther on the Creation, pp. 152f.

where none existed before, and where the state of nature had been quite the contrary. For the whole face of Nature was changed by that mighty convulsion. . . How much excellency has perished from our bodies through sin. Wherefore the sum of the matter under discussion is that we must speak of the whole nature since its corruption, as an entirely altered face of things: a face which nature has assumed, first by means of sin in Adam, and secondly by the awful effects of the universal Deluge. Nor has God ceased to act in the same way. When he punishes sin, he still curses at the same time the earth also.[15]

"The whole world," Luther said elsewhere, "degenerates and grows worse every day."[16] "All creatures, yea, even the sun and the moon, have put on sack cloth."[17]

Calvin had Augustine's (and Isaiah's) feeling for nature. He held, to be sure, that man, without grace, was unable to appreciate nature, but that nature itself remained the evidence to the enlightened of God's goodness:

God . . . hath manifested himself in the formation of every part of the world. . . . On all his works he hath inscribed his glory in characters so clear, unequivocal, and striking, that the most illiterate and stupid cannot exculpate themselves by the plea of ignorance. . . . But therein appears the vile ingratitude of men; that, while they ought to be proclaiming bounties bestowed upon them, they are inflated with greater pride. . . . Notwithstanding the clear representations given by God in the mirror of his works, both of himself and of his everlasting dominion, such is our stupidity that, always inattentive to these obvious testimonies, we derive no advantages from them.[18]

Although Calvin was aware of the tradition according to which the earth originally called "good" by the Creator had been defaced by the Deluge in consequence of mankind's sin, he held to the other in line with Augustine: "Notwithstanding I say that it is the same earth which was created in the beginning."[19]

In seventeenth-century England the positions respectively of Chrysostom and Luther, of Augustine and Calvin were taken in the battle of the books, the controversy between the "Ancients" and "Moderns" by Godfrey Goodman and George Hakewill.[20] Bishop Goodman (d. 1656), set forth the pessimistic view

[15] Luther on the Creation, pp. 164f.; Nicolson, *op. cit.* p. 102.

[16] Nicolson, *op. cit.* p. 102.

[17] Nicolson, *op. cit.* p. 104.

[18] *Institutes,* I, 58, 61, 69; Nicolson, *op. cit.* p. 97.

[19] *Commentaries upon the First Book of Moses Called Genesis,* ed. by John King (Edinburgh, 1847), I, 113f.; 174f.

[20] The controversy was made familiar to scholars by Richard F. Jones in his *Background of the Battle of the Books* (St. Louis, 1920) and in *Ancients and Moderns: A Study of the Rise of Scientific Movement in Seventeenth-Century England* (St. Louis, 1936;1961). See also Victor Harris, *All Coherence Gone* (Chicago, 1949) and Nicolson, *op. cit.,* pp. 105-112. Geoffrey Ingle Soden deals with the controversy in *Godfrey Goodman, Bishop of Gloucester, 1583-1656* (London, 1954), ch. vii.

13

with extraordinary grimness in *The Fall of Man, or The Corruption of Nature proved by the Light of Natural Reason* (London, 1616).[21] Goodman rested his case on a recital of man's miseries for which he is himself responsible. Although the weight of God's wrath which man must carry is preponderant, Goodman held that the whole creation is so closely interwoven that, though without guilt, punishment is visited upon all creation also, man's sin serving as example and precedent: "God at length in his wisdome, for our sins, thought fit to deface it. ' "As man was corrupted . . . so it stood with the uniformities of God's judgments, that nothing should remain untouched, no not the elements themselves."[22]

Although the partly Welsh bishop of Gloucester (who toward the end of his career inwardly converted to Roman Catholicism), remaining Ptolemaic despite the celestial revolution of Nicholas Copernicus (d. 1543), held that even the nine spheres had been adversely affected by Adam's disobedience, he still thought he could hear the music of the spheres and, kindly disposed to the animal world, he was convinced that "for his natural use, for his food, clothing, labour . . . they [the creatures] were appointed [and also] for his spiritual use, to serve him the nature of Chaplaines, while their masters . . . dishonour him [God]." Much such winsome reflection was set forth by Goodman in *The Creatures Praysing God, or the Religion of dumbe creatures* (1622), wherein he wrote:

They are dumbe, therefore they make us their Advocates . . . they are our tongues to set forth Gods praise . . . our praise becomes theirs, and their praise becomes ours; we are their God-fathers to make the confession of their faith; they are our Remembrancers, and serve as the seales of our truth. And thus there is not only a communion of saints, but also a communion of Creatures, which ioyne together in one naturall service of God; as we partake with them in substance, so we ioyne with them or rather learne of them, the commendations of God. . . . [A]s we partake in his [Christ's] Sacrifice, in regard of our nature, the manhood of Christ, so all the Creatures can not be excluded, in regard of one common matter, or substance, in the body of Christ; so that in him in him alone, the whole world, the great world, in the little world, becomes a true and reall sacrifice.[23]

George Hakewill challenged Goodman in an *Apologie of the Power and Providence of God* (1627), in which he argued that sin and decay had not passed from the microcosm to the macrocosm. Insisting that God would not have made the earth corruptible or allowed it to be contaminated by man, Hakewill would recognize only mutability but not decay, not degeneration, not some vast defacement of the globe.

21 Quotations from the second edition of this rare book are to be found in Harris, *op. cit.*, pp. 8-46; Glacken, *op. cit.*, p. 391.

22 Nicolson, *op cit.* p. 108; Soden, *op. cit.*, pp. 79; 85.

23 Goodman, *The Creatures Praysing God*, pp. 21; 27 f.; quoted by Soden in a whole chapter devoted to the work, *op. cit.*, ch. xi.

Goodman in his rebuttal saw in Hakewill a disposition to embrace the Aristotelian-Averroist heresy of the eternity of the world from which he restrained himself only out of traditional piety. Goodman, like Luther, held to the view that the earth when called by God good was the Mundane Egg: "Before the deluge the earth was more level, and framed according to a better rule of a Globe or a Center."[24] If man, being *"nexus* and *naturae vinculum,"* breaks his proper pattern, "it must necessarily follow, that all the rest of the creatures, which were bound and knit together in man, should likewise be inordinate, and overflow their owne banks." Thus all creatures shared in God's original curse of nature and groan under the burden of man's sin. After all, the creatures are wholly designed for man's use, and their suffering cannot be too great if it serves for man's admonition and as a "remembrance of his [own] sinne."[25] The progression from the corruption of man to the corruption of the world, as supported by this unity and symmetry of creation, was, according to Goodman, immediately effected by one simple analogy: man was "the mirrour of nature . . . a little world epitomized, an abridgement of nature," and that which was applicable to man was applicable to the world. Man's violation destroyed the perfect symmetry of the whole; the disobedience of the primordial microcosm set the macrocosm on fire. Goodman, turning toward the end of his *Fall* from the perversity of man to the decay of the world, ruminated on his achievement to this point:

[M]e thinks I have subdued the little world, and brought man as a captive or slave, through much misery and sorrow, at length to the place of his execution; and having now possest my selfe of the fairest fortresse, or tower in nature (man that is a little world), I cannot here content my selfe, but I begin to enquire, whether there are as yet more worlds to be conquered? and behold in the second place, I will fall upon the great world, and I will attempt with Archimedes, to shake her foundations, to threaten her ruine, in this generall corruption and dissolution of man: for this punishment (*morte morieris*) though it principally concernes man, yet the whole world cannot be exempted from it, being directed and ordained onely for mans use, containing in it selfe the very same seedes, and causes of death and destruction; and as it is most fit and agreeable to our present condition, that being corruptible in our selves, we should likewise dwell in houses of corruption.[26]

The scientific community would in due course follow Hakewill and not Goodman.

Outside the scientific circle of Hakewill and later in the same century we encounter an unusually vivid sectarian Christian expression of confidence in

[24] Nicolson, *op. cit.,* p. 108.

[25] Goodman, *The Fall of Man,* pp. 17, 27, 217, 314; quoted in V. Harris, *op. cit.,* pp. 24. The punishment *morte morieris* is, of course, a reference to Satan's deceptive promise in 3: 4 "by death thou shalt not die."

[26] Goodman, *The Fall of Man;* Harris, *op. cit.,* p. 23. Some of Goodman's arguments are printed in the 3rd edition of Hakewill's *Apologie* for refutation (1635).

15

nature. A Quaker, Charles Marshall (d. 1698) explicitly distinguished fallen man and his fallen institutions, including the warring sects, from paradisaic nature untouched by corruption. He took quite literally the scriptural injunction to fly for a season of solace and reflective solitude into the forests and glades. He recalled how before becoming a Quaker he had grown dissatisfied with the Independents and the Baptists, although moved by the "tender" earnestness of their quest; and, feeling burdened with his own sin and the overpowering sense of the fallen state of mankind as a whole over against the humility and guiltless splendor of other creatures, he

became like the solitary desert, and mourned like a dove without a mate. And seeing I could not find the living among the dead professions, I spent much time in retirements alone, in the fields and woods, and by springs of water, which I delighted to lie by, and drink of. . . . And in those days, as I walked and beheld the creation of God Almighty, everything testified against me, heaven and earth, the day and the night . . . , the watercourses and the springs of the great deep, keeping in their respective places: the grass and flowers of the field; the fish of the sea and fowls of the air, keeping their order; but man alone, the chief of the work of God's hand, [I saw was] degenerated.[27]

The feeling for nature as a source of moral refreshment and as a realm capable of independent praise of the Creator persisted well in to the Romantic period.

In eighteenth-century England in Isaac Watts (d. 1748) the capacity of nature to rejoice in creation and to praise the Creator came out in several hymns, notably in the Christmas hymn "Joy to the World" (1719), a paraphrase of Psalm 98: "Let heaven and nature sing."

II. NATURE AS DECAYING OR AS CONSTANT

The second set of scriptural antinomies, or perhaps profound complementarities, is akin to the foregoing scriptural reflections on whether nature is fallen with and because of man. Here, however, the condition of nature is not connected with man's conduct one way or the other. The scriptural set of antinomies is as follows: Nature of its own is decaying or running down to its destruction. *Sed contra:* Nature will remain constant under God's tutelage until the final judgment and the conflagration of the universe or it will actually improve or progress toward the fulfilment of all things according to their intended perfection. Admittedly some of the texts under this second rubric fit rubric *i contra*. But texts on nature for itself deserve special notice; and there are, in fact, a few texts that quite explicitly exculpate nature and they came in the course of Christian thought to be quite influential for a season.

The scriptural *locus classicus* (in this case Apocryphal) for the entropy of

---

[27] *The Journal* of Charles Marshall, printed by Richard Barrett (London, 1844), p. 2.

nature is IV Ezra 5:55: "Consider, therefore, thou also that ye [human beings] are inferior in stature in comparison with your predecessors; and so, also, [will be] your posterity than ourselves: even as creation is already grown old, and is already past the strength of youth." Observe that this decay or decline is not linked with man's disobedience and fall. Compare a kindred text Psalm 102:26: "They [the heavens] will perish, but thou [O God] dost endure; they will wax old as a garment."

The scriptural sanction, in contrast, for the constancy of nature and the mainstay of those Christians in the course of two thousand years of history who would, for scientific purposes among others, like to be able to count on regularity in the natural world was Ecclesiastes 7:10: "Say not thou, what is the cause that the former days are better than these, for thou dost not inquire wisely concerning this." In Psalm 119:10 there is even scriptural sanction for human progress on the basis of revelation and adherence to its prescripts: "I am wiser than the ancients, because I obey thy laws."

Notable exponents of the pessimistic view in pre-Christian classical antiquity were Hesiod, with his theory of human nature and society in successive declensions from an aboriginal golden age, and Lucretius with his theory of the unwinding of nature at large. These two and other classical writers would continue into the seventeenth century and beyond to reinforce the pessimistic scriptural strand to which attention has now been drawn.

A foremost Christian exponent of this pessimistic view, drawing perhaps more on classical sources in this case than Scripture, was Tertullian of Carthage (d. c.220). He wrote:

What more frequently meets our view (and occasions complaints), is our teeming population; our numbers are burdensome to the world, which can hardly supply us its natural elements; our wants grow more and more keen, and our complaints more bitter in all mouths, whilst nature fails in affording us her usual sustenance. In very deed, pestilence, and famine, and wars, and earthquakes have to be regarded as a remedy for nations, as the means of pruning the luxuriousness of the human race.[28]

Another witness to the pessimistic view of nature in decline was Bishop Cyprian of Carthage (d. 258). It was in the context of arguing against the proconsul of Africa, Demetrianus, who had contended that wars, famine, and pestilence then plaguing the Roman world were to be imputed to the Christians for drawing off devotees of the worship of the gods of nature that Cyprian asserted, among other things, that in any case "the world is changing and passing away,"[29] and, therefore, that what Demetrianus complained of was of the order of things unconnected with the spread of Christianity. We can overhear this world-weary sigh from Christian antiquity in the following paragraph:

[28] *De Anima,* 30.
[29] Cyprian, *Treatise* VII, p. 25; *ANF,* V, p. 475.

[Y]ou must in the first place know this, that the world has now grown old, and does not abide in that strength in which it formerly stood; nor has it that vigor and force which it formerly possessed. This, even were we silent; and if we alleged no proofs from the sacred Scriptures and from the divine declarations, the world itself is now announcing, and bearing witness to its decline by the testimony of its failing estate. In the winter there is not such an abundance of showers for nourishing the seeds; in the summer the sun has not so much heat for cherishing the harvest; nor in the spring season are the corn-fields so joyous; nor are the autumnal seasons so fruitful in their leafy products. The layers of marble are dug out in less quantity from the disembowelled and wearied moutains; the diminished quantities of gold and silver suggest the early exhaustion of the metals, and the impoverished veins are straitened and decreased day by day; the husbandman is failing in the fields, the sailor at sea, the soldier in the camp, innocence in the market, justice in the tribunal, concord in friendships, skilfulness in the arts, discipline in morals. This is the sentence passed on the world, this is God's law, that everything that has had a beginning should perish, and things that have grown should become old, and that strong things should become weak, and great things become small, and that, when they have become weakened and diminished, they should come to an end.[30]

Interestingly, another African, the apologist Arnobius of Sicca (d. c. 330), about fifty years after Cyprian, encountering the same pagan argument that Christians were responsible for the current calamities of natural and human history, argued in a manner just the opposite of Cyprian, denying that the heavens or the earth and its life had in any way deteriorated. He rejoiced, in contrast, at the very constancy of nature. Repudiating the conclusion of Lucretius' *De rerum natura* Arnobius asked in eloquent self-confidence as to the constancy and essential goodness of nature:

Has the construction of this massive mechanism which covers us all and in which we are held enclosed in any way been shaken or destroyed? . . .
Have the winds ceased to blow? And have their blasts died down so that the sky is not gathered together into clouds and the fields do not submit to be moistened by the storms? Does the earth refuse to receive the seeds entrusted to it or are the trees unwilling to leaf out? Has the flavor in edible fruits or the vine with its juices been changed? Is foul gore squeezed out from the olive berries and has the lamp, gone out, lost its source of supply?
Do the animals accustomed to the land and those that pass their life in the seas have no mating season? Do they fail to protect, each according to its own habits and its own law of instinct, the young which they have generated in their wombs?
Finally, do men themselves, whom the first creation scattered over the habitable shore, not contract marriages with the proper nuptial rites? Do they not beget children they love most dearly? Do they not carry on public and private and family business? Do they not, as each pleases, direct their talents to varied arts and different kinds of learning, and reap the profits of their cleverness and zeal?[31]

Graeco-Roman society, when Arnobius wrote these optimistic words about

[30] Cyprian, *Treatise* V, p. 3; *op. cit.*, p. 458.

[31] Arnobius, *The Case Against the Pagans*, I, p. 2; George McCracken, tr., *Ancient Christian Writers*, I (Westminster, 1949), pp. 59f.

mankind and nature, was still more than half pagan for he was writing about the world in general and not expressly about Christians.

The opposite patristic views respectively of Fathers Cyprian and Arnobius as to whether nature is declining or remains constant reappeared in intense debate in seventeenth-century England. It was, as we have already seen, one important aspect of the quarrel between "the Ancients" and "the Moderns."[32] The pessimistic view of the Ancients was something of an inhibition of the rising natural sciences for two reasons: 1) it presumed the superiority of the natural scientists and philosophers of antiquity, compared to whom the seventeenth-century scholars should feel themselves dwarfed as by classical giants, and 2) it also suggested that even present-day specimens of natural history were runtish and in other ways inferior to what the classical observers had described.

A morose expression of the view of Cyprian with some resonances from him and his scriptural sources, updated to 1580, is that of the obscure English divine Francis Shakelton (d. 1631):

> Let this therefore be a forcible argument to prove, that the world shall have an ende: for so muche as it doeth waxe old, and every part thereof doeth feele some debilitie and weaknesse. For there is lesse vertue in Plantes, and hearbes then ever before. And more feeble strength in every living creature then ever was before. It remaineth therefore (of necessitie) that shortly there shall be an ende and consummation of the Worlde, because it is (as it were) subjecte to olde age, and therefore feeble in every parte.[33]

The idea of nature's inevitable decay likewise appealed to the Anglican divine and Metaphysical poet, John Donne (d. 1631), who made extravagant use of the classical-scriptural theme in *An Anatomie of the World: The First Anniversary* (1611), weaving it in and out of his metaphysical conceits. In a sermon preached in 1625, he declared:

As the world is the whole frame of the world, God hath put into it a reproofe, a rebuke (lest it should seem eternall) . . . [namely], a sensible decay and age in the whole frame of the world, and every piece thereof. The seasons of the year irregular and distempered; the Sun fainter, and languishing; men lesse in stature, and shorter-lived. No addition, but only every yeare, new sorts, new species of wormes, and flies, and sicknesses, which argue more and more putrefaction of which they are engendered. . . . S. Cyprian observed this in his time, when writing to Demetrianus, who imputed all those calamities which afflicted the world then to the impiety of the Christians who would not joyne with them in the worship of their gods, Cyprian went no farther for the cause of these calamities, but *Ad senescentem mundum*, To the age and impotency of the whole world.[34]

[32] Jones and Harris, *op. cit.*

[33] *A blazyng Starre or burnyng Beacon, seene the 10 October last* (London, 1580) sig. Aiiii - Av; quoted by Jones, *op. cit.*, p. 24.

[34] Sermon XXXVI of the edition of 1640; quoted by Jones, *op. cit.*, p. 25. The already cited incisive *The Fall of Man, or the Corruption of Nature* by Bishop Goodman also fits here.

Expressly attacking this melancholy view of nature, notably as articulated anciently by Cyprian and currently by John Dunne and Bishop Goodman, was the already mentioned George Hakewill (1578-1649). He had studied abroad, notably at Heidelberg, had been named chaplain to Prince Charles, a doctor of divinity and archdeacon in Surrey. The long title of his book in 1627 summarizes his concern:

An Apologie of the Power and Providence of God in the Government of the World. Or an Examination and Censure of the Common Errour Touching Natures Perpetuall and Universall Decay, Divided into Foure Bookes: Whereof the first treates of this pretended decay in generall, together with some preparatives thereunto. The second of the pretended decay of the Heavens and Elements, together with that of the elementary bodies, man only excepted. The third of the pretended decay of mankinde in regard of age and duration, of strength and stature, of arts and wits. The fourth of this pretended decay in matters of manners, together with a large proofe of the future consummation of the World from the testimony of the Gentiles, and the uses which we are to draw from the consideration thereof (Oxford, 1627).

Hakewill's concern was to vindicate scientific inquiry into natural and human history without the debilitating effects of the melancholy view going back in the Christian line, at least, as far as Cyprian. As a Christian, Hakewill felt that he could be most effective in piercing his opponents with quills taken from Scripture and the Church Fathers. The title-page text of the *Apologie* carries the already cited verse from Ecclesiastes; and he adduced further in favor of the constancy of nature, Minucius Felix, Tertullian, Lactantius, the already quoted Arnobius,[35] Eusebius of Caesarea, Augustine, and even Cyprian[36] in a different mood.

A contemporary, John Jonston of Poland, drawing heavily on Hakewill, will set forth the common thesis of religious men in science in *The Constancy of Nature* (1632).

In Venice the Abbot Secondo Lancelotti of Perugia a few years earlier also refuted the idea that "the world is more miserable and malicious and fuller of vice than anciently" and denied that there ever had been an age any more golden than the present in *L'Hoggidi, overo il mondo non peggiore ne piu calamitoso del passato* (Venice, 1627).[37]

This seventeenth-century debate was not resolved by its participants. The view of the "Ancients" did not merge with that of the "Moderns" until later naturalists described the constancy of inexorable laws of nature above or behind the mutation of species and the inconstancy or flux of all forms of being

---

[35] Quoted at length in 1630 edition, pp. 60-65, being from *The Case Against the Pagans*, I, pp. 1-16.

[36] George Hakewill, *An Apologie of the Power* . . . (Oxford, 1627), p. 47.

[37] Summarized by Hakewill in the second edition of his *Apologie*, 1630.

whether of society, of life, or of creation at large. The nineteenth-century Darwinists indeed acknowledged the inconstancy or mutability of nature "red in tooth and claw," noted by the "Ancients," but social Darwinists proceeded to reverse the implications for human society, at least, in the direction of progress for mankind.

A last echo of the specific phrases of the controversy between the Ancients and the Moderns may be that in the work of the Andover Congregationalist liberal George Harris (d. 1922), *Moral Evolution* (Boston, 1896): "By distant contrast, the moderns are better than the ancients. The retrospect which sobers also animates. . . . Optimism is more than a hope for the future."[38]

Since this evolutionary progressivism has informed much of modern thought, even Christian thought, it has until quite recently been difficult for historians to empathize with the brooding pessimism of the defenders of the "Ancients" in the English seventeenth century or with their still earlier counterparts in the age of the medieval Schoolmen and that of the ancient Church Fathers. Yet scriptural pessimism and Darwinian realism with respect to nature have been in one guise or another a major thrust in Christian civilization, even though its ascetic *contemptus mundi* actually drew more on this question from Plato and Paul than from Jesus and Isaiah.

With our rising sense of alarm about the world-wide effects of pollutants like DDT on the photosynthesis of plankton in the oceans and like nuclear fallout and even thermonuclear radiation on genetic mutation with attendant frustration of the reproductive process in all living things, contemporary readers can at least understand sympathetically both sides of the conflict between the "Moderns" and the "Ancients" and still take comfort from the nature parables of Jesus and the cosmic visions of Isaiah.

III. NATURE AS A DISTINCTIVE CREATION FOR ITS OWN SAKE AND FOR THE PRAISE OF ITS CREATOR: OR NATURE AS THE REALM OF MAN'S STEWARDSHIP OR EXPLOITATION

A third set of scriptural antinomies influential in Christian history is as follows: Nature is the realm of the dominion of man, whether as steward, or exploiter, or as mediator between God and creation. *Sed contra:* Nature is not wholly for man and as an independent expression of the plenitude of divine creativity sings praises to the Creator and can supply man with emblems and evidences of the Creator apart from revealed Scripture. It is this set of scriptural passages that most people have in mind when they refer to the scriptural component in the ecological crisis.

---

38 *Op. cit.*, p. 445; cf. *A Century's Change in Religion* (Boston, 1914), pp. 180ff.

The scriptural *loci classici* for the anthropocentric views of the creaturely world are, of course, Genesis 1:27f.: "So God created man in his own image . . . male and female. And God said to them: 'Be fruitful and multiply, and fill the earth and subdue it; and have dominion . . . over every living thing;' " and, after the Deluge, Genesis 9:1f.: "And God blessed Noah and his sons and said to them: 'Be fruitful and multiply, and fill the earth. The fear of you and the dread of you shall be upon every beast of the earth, and upon every bird of the air, upon everything that creeps on the ground and all the fish of the sea; *into your hands they are delivered!*" Even more influential is the equivalent version in Psalm 8:6f.: "Thou hast given him dominion over the works of thy hands; thou hast put all things under his feet, all sheep and oxen, and also the beasts of the field, the birds of the air, and the fish of the sea, whatever passes along the paths of the sea."

The scriptural sanctions for the more comprehensive view of nature as independently of concern to God are in the New Testament, the nature parables and allusions of Jesus to the birds of the air and lilies of the field (Matthew 6). From the Old Testament several texts came to be cited in Christian history in sanction of the relative autonomy of nature: Proverbs 8:30, where Wisdom, as the instrumental artificer of creation, speaks: "[T]hen was I with him [God], like a master workman; and I was daily his delight, rejoicing before him always" and hyperbolic Isaiah 55:12: "[T]he mountains and the hills before you shall break forth into singing, and all the trees of the field shall clap their hands." In the same vein is Psalm 98:8f.: "Let the floods clap their hands; let the hills sing for joy together before the Lord, for he comes to rule the earth. He will judge the world with righteousness, and the peoples with equity." Admittedly these three last texts speak either of creation before the fall or of nature at the eschatological moment of man's redemption, but in the course of Christian history when Christians wished to give expression to the glory and joy of nature between Creation and the Eschaton they resorted to these texts for sanction.

The most extraordinary and explicit formulation of the anthropocentric view of nature is that of the otherwise universalistic Origen of Alexandria and Caesarea (d. c. 254). In refuting the pagan Celsus, who was very well read in Christian literature and had observed that Christians thought of themselves as the very center of creation, as though the sun and the seasons and all the rest were not so much for ants and bees as for the teeming ghettoes of human squalor, Origen replied:

Celsus, being muddle-headed, did not see that he is also criticizing the Stoic school of philosophers. They quite rightly put man and the rational nature in general above all irrational beings, and say that providence has made everything primarily for the sake of rational nature. Rational beings which are the primary things have the value of children who are born; whereas irrational and inanimate things have that of the *afterbirth* which is created with the child.[39] . . . The Creator, then, has made everything to serve the rational being and his natural intelligence.[40]

Origen went on to detail the obvious uses for man of dogs and even the wild animals that "exercise" in him "the seeds of courage." Elsewhere he became more reflective about the plenitude and mystery of creation:

> There are things in creation hard to understand, or even indiscoverable for human beings. We are not in consequence to condemn the Creator of the universe just because we cannot discover the reason for the creation of scorpions or other venomous beasts. The right thing for a man, who is aware of the weakness of our race and who knows it is impossible to understand the reasons of God's design even when most minutely examined, is to ascribe the knowledge of these things to God, who will later on, if we are judged worthy, reveal to us the matters about which we are now reverently in doubt.[41]

The anthropocentric view was also taken but in a very comprehensive and stewardly sense by Nemesius, bishop of Emesa in Syria (late fourth century), who wrote the oldest extant threatise *On Human Nature* (*Peri physeos anthrópou*), quite consciously accommodating the Greek philosophical and the scriptural traditions. Herein he developed in the Christian context what has been traced elsewhere as the concept of the great chain of being,[42] defining man as "on the boundary" between what Nemesius called "the intelligible order and the phenomenal order." Thus the oldest Christian anthropological threatise happens to stress man's mediatorship in the universe rather than his potential dominion over it:

> It is well known that man has some things in common with the inanimate creatures, and shares life with the plant and animal creation, while partaking intelligence in common with all beings endowed with reason. With inanimate things he shares a material body mingled of the four elements. With plants he shares not only this but also the faculties of self-nutriment and generation. With irrational animals he shares all these things, and in addition, a range of voluntary movements, together with the faculties of appetite, anger, feeling and respiration. All these things man and the irrational animals have in common, if not everywhere on equal

[39] Origen, *Contra Celsum*, IV, ch. 74.

[40] *Ibid.*, ch. 78.

[41] *Selectio in Psalm;* Philocalia ii; quoted by Wallace Hadrill, *op. cit.*, p. 114.

[42] Arthur O. Lovejoy, *The Great Chain of Being*, (Cambridge, 1957), p. 59 where he defines the chain thus: "The result was the conception of the plan and structure of the world which, through the Middle Ages and down to the late eighteenth century, many philosophers, most men of science, and, indeed, most educated men, were to accept without question – the conception of the universe as a 'Great Chain of Being,' composed of an immense, or – by the strict but seldom rigorously applied logic of the principle of continuity – of an infinite, number of links ranging in hierarchical order from the meagerest kind of existents, which barely escape non-existence, through 'every possible' grade up to the *ens perfectissimum* – or, in a somewhat more orthodox version, to the highest possible kind of creature, between which and the Absolute Being the disparity was assumed to be infinite – every one of them differing from that immediately above and that immediately below it by the 'least possible' degree of difference."

terms. Finally, by being rational, man shares with the incorporeal rational intelligences the prerogative of applying, to whatever he will, reason, understanding, and judgement. So he pursues virtues, and follows after godliness, in which the quest of every several virtue finds its goal.

It follows from these considerations that man's being is on the boundary between the intelligible order and the phenomenal order. As touching his body and its faculties, he is on a par with the irrational animate, and with the inanimate, creatures. As touching his rational faculties he claims kinship, as we said, with incorporeal beings. It would seem that the Creator linked up each several order of creation with the next, so as to make the whole universe one and akin.

We may see herein the best proof that the whole universe is the creation of one God. For not only has he united all particular things in making them members of one order of reality, but he has made them fit together, each to each.[43]

The oldest extant Christian treatise on nature in general was *Peri physeōs*, by Dionysius the Great, bishop of Alexandria (d. c. 264). It survives only in a fragment, was apparently so intent upon challenging the random atomism of Epicurus that it made no special claim to an anthropocentric universe, and was content to insist that the heavens and man alike came into being by God's providential handiwork:

> Or who can endure to hear that this great house, which consists of heaven and earth, and, because of the great and manifold wisdom displayed upon it, is called the Cosmos, has been set in order by atoms drifting with no order at all, and that disorder has thus become order? . . . . But if there were neither word, nor choice, nor order of ruler laid upon them, but they by themselves directing themselves through the great throng of the stream, and passing out through the great tumult of their collisions, were brought together like to like not by the guidance of God, as the poet[44] says, but ran together and gathered in groups recognizing their own kin, then wonderful surely would be this democracy of the atoms, friends welcoming and embracing one another, and hastening to settle in one common home; while some of them rounded themselves off of their own accord into that mighty luminary the sun, in order to make day, and others flamed up into many pyramids perhaps of stars, in order to crown the whole heaven; while others are ranged around, perchance to make it firm, and throw an arch over the ether for the luminaries to ascend, and that the confederacies of the common atoms may choose their own abodes, and portion out the heaven into habitations and stations for themselves.[45]

We here adduce Bishop Dionysius simply as an exponent of creative purposiveness in the universe, since the extant fragment is inconclusive as to whether he viewed nature beyond humankind as purposive apart from man.

Expressly non-anthropocentric was our acquaintance Arnobius, (above Set

---

[43] *On the Nature of Man*, 2; tr. by William Telfer, Library of Christian Classics, IV, p. 228.

[44] Lucretius (d. 55 B.C.), *De rerum natura*.

[45] *De natura* survives as a fragment *apud* Eusebius, *Praeparatio Evangelii*, chs. xxiii - xxvii; the foregoing translation is that of Edwin H. Gifford, two volumes (Oxford, 1903), II, pp. 835, 837.

1) who in his *Case Against the Pagans* was quite explicit that Christians should not be self-centered in their interpretation of creation:

What if – and this is nearest the truth – what seems adverse to us is not really evil to the world itself, and that judging all things in terms of our own advantage, we blame the results of nature because of unproved opinions? . . . Would you have us say, then, that the clouds hang over the sky with an injurious covering because one cannot at his ease tan his skin to his taste and provide an excuse for drinking bouts? All these events which take place and happen under this mass of the universe are not for our creature comforts but should be regarded as in the arrangements and plans of nature itself. . . .

Hellebore is a poison to men: ought it for this reason not grow? The wolf lies in wait at sheepfolds: is nature at all to blame because it has created a beast most dangerous to the woolbearer? By its bite the serpent takes away life: would you really condemn the foundation of things because it added to living creatures monsters so fierce? . . . .

Therefore, if you wish your complaints to have a place for consideration, you must, my good men, first tell us whence and who you are; whether the world was produced and fashioned for you, or whether you have come into it, as tenants hailing from other regions. And seeing that it is not in your power to say, and you cannot explain for what cause you live beneath this vault of heaven, stop thinking anything belongs to you, since those things which take place take place not for the benefit of one individual but arise for the good of the whole.[46]

Augustine was likewise quite clearly on the side of the relative autonomy of nature with its own divinely intended purpose apart from man:

Therefore, it is not with respect to our convenience or discomfort, but with respect to their own nature, that the creatures are glorifying their Artificer.[47]

In a sermon to the people Augustine declared:

Ask the loveliness of the earth, ask the loveliness of the sea, ask the loveliness of the wide airy spaces, ask the loveliness of the sky, ask the order of the stars, ask the sun making the day light with its beams, ask the moon tempering the darkness of the night that follows, ask the living things which move in the waters, which tarry on the land, which fly in the air; ask the souls that are hidden, the bodies that are perceptive; the visible things which must be governed, the invisible things which govern – ask all these things, and they will all answer thee, Lo, see we are lovely. Their loveliness is their confession. And these lovely but mutable things, who has made them, save Beauty immutable?[48]

Under the rubric of the stewardship of man over nature over against the autonomy of nature, we must pay our respects to Francis of Assisi (d. 1226). He undoubtedly in his own right and in the subsequent interpretation of his mission by devout Franciscans played a pivotal role in the shift in the attitude toward nature that many have in modern times drawn attention to. But although Francis

[46] Arnobius, i, 9-12; *op. cit.*, pp. 66-68.

[47] Augustine, *City of God*, XII.

[48] "Sermones ad Populum," 2d series, No. 241, ch. ii, par. 2, *Oeuvres Complètes de St. Augustin*, 18, p. 238; quoted by Glacken, *op. cit.*, p. 200.

was a brother of his fellow creatures, he was also in another sense their prelapsarian Adamic steward, holding spiritual dominion over them by virtue of his propertylessness and his Christ-like obedience to God. Francis, in glorying in his fellow creatures, led to the almost revolutionary view of the brotherhood or kinship of human beings with the flora and fauna and indeed the heavenly orbs as alike fellow creatures under God, Creator and Father. We but recall St. Francis' famous canticle:

> Praised be the Lord my God
> By Messer Sun, my brother above all,
> Who by his rays lights us and lights the day—
> Radiant is he, with his great splendour stored,
> Thy glory, Lord, confessing.
> By Sister Moon and Stars my Lord is praised,
> Where clear and fair they in the heavens are raised
> Radiant is he, with his great splendour stored,
> Where clear and fair they in the heavens are raised. . . .
> Praised be my Lord by (*per*) our sister, Mother Earth.[49]

Though this sense of the fraternity with fellow creatures was the most distinctive achievement of Francis — and this was continued in the Franciscan Minister General and schoolman Bonaventure (d. 1274) with his own affirmation of "the smallest creatures as his brothers" — still it must be recognized that Francis as the imitator of Jesus even unto stigmatism was preeminently the New Man, the renewed second Adam, and as such the gentle husbandman in the garden of creation, preaching to the birds, covenanting with the fierce wolf, but he still commanded nature; for Francis' love of nature was grounded, as the *Vita prima* of Thomas of Celano suggests, in his having been set free to bring not only men but also irrational creation from groaning and travail into the freedom of the sons of God.[50] Yet by understanding the truest sons of God to be those unencumbered by possessions and hence by any rules but those over self in order to serve others in imitation of Christ, Francis brought many Franciscans, Poor Clares, and Tertiaries very close to the ideal of the anxiety-free birds of the air and lilies of the field (Matt. 6:26; 28f.). In St. Francis in effect two of our types of attitudes towards nature have coalesced.

---

[49] Il Cantico di Frate Sole is officially entitled *Laudes creaturarum* (The Praises of/by the Creatures). Ambiguous in the Italian throughout the Canticle is the crucial preposition *per*, which could mean either that God is praised *for* the creatures (sun, moon, wind, earth with her diverse fruits, grasses, and flowers, forgiving and meek persons, and sister death) or that God is praised *by* the creatures. The translation above reads *per* in the latter sense, as a *Benedicite*, as does the official title in Latin. John Moorman favors this reading, *A History of the Franciscan Order from its Origins to the Year 1517* (Oxford, 1968), p. 76. The original is printed in *Speculum Perfectionis*, ed. by L. Lemmen (Quaracchi, 1901), 140; L. Todi dealt monographically with the *Cantico* (Todi, 1925).

[50] *Vita prima*, lib. i, cap. 29, pp. 80-81; *Analecta Franciscana*, X, pp. 59-61.

The Dominican Thomas Aquinas, untouched by the Franciscan feeling for nature, restated definitively in his *Summa Theologiae* the basic idea of creation as being solely for man when he wrote, "... the life of animals and plants is preserved not for themselves but for man."[51]

The doctrine of man's dominion over the rest of the created order was emphatically restated in classical Protestantism. But it was also recast in pessimistic terms because of the great stress upon the fall of Adam and original sin. Martin Luther, for example, in his *Lectures on Genesis* went so far as to say that "we retain the name and word 'dominion' as a bare title, but the substance itself has been almost entirely lost."[52] He could look back to prelapsarian Adam and Eve who even in their "bare flesh" were given the rule over all creatures and "insight into all the dispositions of all animals, into their characters and all their powers," and an intuitive knowledge of the astronomy, but Luther could only conclude that all that faculty was now "utterly beyond repair in this life;" and he held that only an approximation to those prelapsarian powers was now possible, "no longer by the dominion which Adam had but through industry and skill ... cunning and deceit."[53]

Both Martin Luther and John Calvin were, however, sensible of the beauty or majesty of nature, particularly the heavens. Luther, for his part, though he ignored the Alps as he passed through them to Rome in 1510, did, as a musician love the birds in the forest canopy below the Wartburg where he worked *incognito* (1521-22). And he drew widely upon natural history in his sermons. Calvin's *Institutes* at certain points are a majestic commentary on Paul's natural theology in Romans and in Acts (Mars Hill address). But Luther and Calvin so sensed the gravity of man's fallen nature that they, in effect, gave strong sanction to the elect, in whatever precarious hold they retained, to implement their dominion over themselves and the natural order.

IV. NATURE AS BENIGNANT OR NATURE AS MALIGN

The fourth set of scriptural antinomies woven into Western history is as follows: Nature is benignant or, to the contrary, nature is malign. Stated otherwise: Nature as the wilderness or desert is the realm or place of renewal, of consolation, of refreshment, of refuge, of retreat, of revelation, of covenantal renewal, of redemption. *Sed contra:* Nature is the wilderness or desert of sands or many waters, the abyss of chaos, the enemy and the haunt of the enemy, the abode of the primordial sea serpent and of Satan himself, and his minions the

---

51 Thomas Aquinas, *Summa*, Q. xcvi, a, 1, 2; also Q lxvi, a, 2.

52 *Luther's Works*, American ed., edited by Jaroslav Pelikan, I (St. Louis, 1958), p. 67.

53 *Ibid.*, pp. 66f.

fiery spirits, snakes, scorpions, and devilish vermin. Of the several scriptural *loci classici* for the favorable role of nature as wilderness we may adduce Jeremiah 2:2: "I [Yahweh] remember the devotion of your youth, your love as a bride, how you followed me in the wilderness, in a land not sown." For the counter-vailing view there is the Old Testament fear of the awesome primordial waters on which God's creation precariously rests: Psalm 24:2: "For he has founded it upon the floods." There are innumerable Old Testament texts substantiating the view of the desert as evil and accursed. For the New Testament the capital text is, of course, Matthew 4:1: "Then Jesus was led up by the Spirit into the wilderness to be tempted by the devil."

There are, as one may sense from the doubled statement of these opposites, two aspects to the contrasting themes we now take up. There is first of all the distinctively Hebraic experience, documented in the Old Testament, with the contrasting terrains of the wilderness and the agricultural lands. All peoples of the Fertile Crescent feared and suffered from the desert and parching drought. The Israelites were one with them in this hate or fear of the desert and also in their interest in pastures, orchards, and sown fields. But unlike all the other peoples in the Middle East their own formative history had been shaped by momentous experiences precisely in the desert, beginning with the redemptive sojourn in the Sinai desert and its revelation of the Law. Again and again individual prophets or other ascetics and whole groups, the last of them being the Essenes in Qumran, withdrew into the wilderness for spiritual and ethical purposes and were thereby sensitized to interpret droughts and rains, literally and also spiritually, as acts of divine chastisement or blessing. Accordingly, the Old Testament is replete with attempts to spiritualize geography. At the same time, and this is the second special consideration with respect to nature in the Old Testament, the basic thrust of the martial, the prophetic, and in part the priestly tradition of ancient Israel was directed against the *baalim* of nature and fertility of the indigenous Canaanites; and hence the Lord God of Hosts was usually understood to be several removes from agriculture, the Creator indeed of heaven and earth, but whose austere worship was most characteristically associated with the nomads' portable ark and tabernacle in the desert rather than with a betempled grove, grotto, or mountain shrine. Thus, though there is a persistent suspicion of fecund nature in the Old Testament, the desert as a chaste or sparse form of nature had, in fact, a very religious role.[54]

Within this scriptural tradition the first to dare, given the traditional Hebraic reserve with respect to fecund nature, to call her fostering mother was the Hellenistic Jew, Philo of Alexandria (d. c. 50 A.D.), who declared in one place:

---

[54] See my *Wilderness and Paradise in Christian Thought: The Biblical Experience of the Desert in the History of Christianity and the Paradise Theme in the Theological Idea of the University* (New York: Harper and Rowe, 1962).

"For this was long ago agreed upon among the most approved of the learned men of former days . . . that nature is the mother of the irrational creatures, but the step-mother of men."[55] It will be centuries before Mother Nature would appear in the writings of even nominal Christians. But the equivalent was there from the start and in language both congenial to and shaped partly by Philo in the concept of the seminal Logos or the instrument of God in the creation of the world, which Christians early understood as the pre-incarnational stage in the cosmic career of Jesus Christ and which they came readily to personalize as the eternally engendered Son of God.

Justin Martyr (d. 165) of Rome and earlier of Samaria introduced into Christian thought the Stoic idea of "the seminal Word" or the Word disseminated among all men, "the Logos that was in them."[56] Eventually, Christian thinkers would be able to carry the doctrine of the *Logos spermatikos* from the doctrine of man into their conception of creation and therein have a basis for a sense of intimacy with the created order without being tempted to worship it pantheistically.

A theologically profound and prophetically perceived subsidiary theme under rubric iii is that recurrently nature as the wilderness can be converted by God's grace into a garden and the garden may become a blasted wilderness. In the mysterious transactions of God with man, providentially, mystically, eschatologically, nature as the wilderness can be converted by God's grace into a garden. Contrariwise, the garden of Eden can be converted into a blasted or chastening or ennobling wilderness. The scriptural *locus classicus* for the conversion of desert to garden is Isaiah 35:1: "The wilderness and the dry land shall be glad, the desert shall rejoice and blossom like the rose." Its opposite is Joel 2:3: "The land is like the garden of Eden before them, but after them a desolate wilderness" because of the hot glow of God's punishment.

Christians came literally to seek out the wilderness or desert for contemplation and refuge. Eusebius of Caesarea (d. c. 340), Father of Church History, lived long enough to realize that there were to be as many temptations, vexations, and murmurings under the Christian Moses, Constantine, as under the former Moses. And many Christians, some of them the most conscientious, began to flee the so-called Christian empire. It was among the hermits and monks that the biblical sense of the ambiguity of the wilderness of Sinai and the wilderness of Jordan lived on, the wilderness of temptation and the wilderness which is a provisional paradise with saints and beasts in harmony, obedient unto Christ.

---

[55] Philo, *On the Posterity of Cain and his Exile*, 162; Loeb Classical Library. Cf. "mother of mankind, nature," *Dec.*, 41; Grant, *op. cit.*, p. 15.

[56] II *Apology*, ch. xiii.

The flight of the hermits into the desert was, for them, a new exodus from bondage. Basil the Great (d. c. 379), the organizer of Eastern monasticism, spoke for the whole company of those who fled into the desert when, before his elevation to the episcopal throne in Caesarea in Cappadocia, he wrote:

I am living . . . in the wilderness wherein the Lord dwelt. Here is the oak of Mamre; here is the ladder which leads to heaven, and the encampments of the angels which Jacob saw; here is the wilderness where the people, purified, received the law, and then going into the land of promise beheld God. Here is Mount Carmel where Elijah abode and pleased God. Here is the plain whither Ezra [IV:14:37-38] withdrew [for forty days], and at God's bidding poured forth from his mouth all his divinely inspired books. Here is the wilderness where the blessed John ate locusts and preached repentance to men. Here is the Mount of Olives, which Christ ascended and there prayed, teaching us how to pray. Here is Christ, the lover of the wilderness; for He says (Matthew 18:20), "Where there are two or three gathered in My name, *there* am I in the midst of them [!]." Here is the narrow and strait way that leadeth to life. Here are teachers and prophets, "wandering in deserts, in mountains, and in dens, and in caves of the earth" (Heb. 11:38). Here are apostles and evangelists and the life of monks, citizens of the desert.[57]

Basil gives us elsewhere a magnificent description of his retreat and is distinctive in praising the beauty not merely of the pastoral countryside but here also the awesome wilds:

There is a high mountain covered with a thick forest, watered on its northerly side by cool and transparent streams. At its base is outstretched an evenly sloping plain, ever enriched by moisture from the mountain. A forest of many-colored and multifarious trees, a spontaneous growth surrounding the place, acts almost as a hedge to enclose it, so that even Calypso's isle, which Homer seems to have admired above all others for itself, is insignificant in comparison with this. . . . Why need I mention the exhalations from the land, or the breezes from the river? Someone else might well marvel at the multitudes of the flowers or of the song of birds; but I have not the leisure to turn my thoughts to these. The highest praise, however, which I can give to the place is that, although it is well adapted by its admirable situation to producing fruits of every kind, for me the most pleasing fruit it nourishes is tranquillity, not only because it is far removed from the disturbances of the city, but also because it attracts not even a wayfarer, except the guests who join me in hunting. For besides its other excellencies, it abounds in game, not those bears and wolves of yours; but it feeds herds of deer and wild goats, hares and animals like these.[58]

Jerome (c. 342-420), translator of the Vulgate from the Hebrew and Greek, may be taken as a representative Latin theorist of the monastic flight into the wilderness. Jerome reworked a number of the desert themes. Writing about the efficacy of baptism, he spoke of Eden, of the Red Sea as a figure of baptism, of the dragons of the deep, of the adders and scorpions that haunt dry places and "behave as if rabid or insane" when brought near water (forever sanctified by

---

[57] Epistle XLIII, ed. and tr. by Roy J. Deferrari, Loeb Library, *Letters*, I, 261. The passage was quoted in my *Wilderness*, p. 39.

[58] Ep. xiv, ed. Deferrari, pp. 106 ff.

Christ in the Jordan). In his famous Epistle CXXV he, like Basil, traced the lineage of Christian monasticism into biblical times and went on to intertwine the wilderness and paradisaic themes we have noted:

He [John the Baptist] lived in the desert, and seeking Christ with his eyes, refused to look at anything else. His rough garb, his girdle made of skins, his diet of locusts and wild honey were all alike designed to encourage virtue and continence. The sons of the prophets, who were the monks of the Old Testament, built for themselves huts by the waters of Jordan and forsaking the crowded cities lived in these on pottage and wild herbs (II Kings 4:38 f.; 6:1 f.). As long as you are at home, *make your cell your paradise*, gather there the varied fruits of Scripture, let this be your favourite companion, and take its precepts to your heart. . . . The sons of Jonadab, we are told, drank neither wine nor strong drink and dwelt in tents pitched wherever night overtook them (Jeremiah 35:6 f.). Others may think what they like and follow each his own bent. But to me a town is a prison and a solitude, paradise. Why do we long for the bustle of cities, we whose very name (*monachus*) speaks of loneliness? To fit him for the leadership of the Jewish people Moses was trained for forty years in the wilderness (Acts 7:29 f.), and it was not till after these that the shepherd of sheep became the shepherd of men.[59]

With the barbarian invasions and the breakdown of the universal Empire, well into the Middle Ages, Graeco-Roman Christians scarcely had dominion over themselves, to say nothing of the barbarian pillage and the reversion to wilderness all about them. In this era and beyond the monks in various groupings continued the ascetic ideal of the hermitage or monastery as an outcropping of paradisaic self-discipline and obedience in the wilderness of the world. There is a sustained ambiguity about the attitude of the ascetics toward their natural environment. On the one hand the fierce or noxious beasts and other creatures were thought of as obstacles to be withstood or overcome like the fomenting figments of their imagination. On the other hand the wildlife about the hermits were signs of Paradise. The ascetics, having achieved an inner harmony and saintly other-worldliness, communicated a calm and loving spirit toward the beasts and birds about them; and monastic chronicles and saints' lives, particularly of the Celtic and Anglo-Saxon missionary and penitential pilgrims, are filled with accounts of the holy harmony between man and beast, often in mutual succor. St. Jerome, with his lion, replaced Androcles as a symbol of harmony of the monastic paradise amid the wilderness.

Successive reformations of monastic communities found themselves hiving like bees in the wilds, converting the wilderness sites into monastic gardens of disciplined spirit: the Cistercians, the Camaldolesi, the Premonstratensians, the Carmelites. The idea of the monastic and eventually also of the sectarian church as the woman fleeing for protection to the wilderness (Rev. 12:6) was an increasingly important motif.[60]

[59] Ep. LXIX, 7, 8; *NPF*, VI, 246 f.

[60] George H. Williams, *The Radical Reformation*, (Philadelphia, 1962), pp. 57-64.

Cistercian Abbot Joachim of Flora (d. 1202) of aristocratic birth, calling himself a *homo agricola a juventute mea* (probably in allusion to the rustic prophet in Zechariah 13:5), sought the wilderness for himself in a stricter rule, escaping into the mountainous wastes of Calabria. There, among other works, he produced in commentary on Revelation his conception of the Eternal Gospel (Rev. 14:6). He took the epoch-making step of identifying the church (woman) of the wilderness in Revelation 12:6 eschatologically and developed an elaborate theology of history in terms of three partly overlapping dispensations of the three Persons of the Trinity. For Joachim, the world was not growing older but younger: the age of the patriarchs under God the Father led into the age of maturity with its celibate clerical Church under God the Son and his vicar the Pope, soon to give way to the age of the monks of the wilderness, the *Ecclesia spiritualis*, foreseen by the Seer of the Apocalypse in the woman with child fleeing into the wilderness.

The followers of Peter Waldo (d. 1217), the Waldensians, eventually fleeing to the fastnesses of the Alps, came likewise to see in their conventicles in the caves the wilderness church of Revelation 12:6.

The monastic and sectarian retreat to the wilderness, the interpretation of it as a provisional paradise, the taming of the wild beasts by the saintly hermits and monks, the conversion of the contemplation of the external wilderness into the mystical wilderness and hence garden of delights,[61] is a persistent thrust in Christian history, and the motif did not remain confined to hermits, monks, and friars, but it even survived in altered forms in much of sectarian and comtemplative Protestantism.

Though passing by the great Schoolmen and the Reformers, the writer cannot forego sharing one sixteenth-century variant of the monastic-wilderness motif in lay form. It is from the *Lament of the Wild Men about the Unfaithful World*, composed by Hans Sachs of Nuremberg (much later converted by Richard Wagner in *Die Minnesänger* into a naturist). Sachs was a Christian primitivist when he wrote this:

> Now since the world is thus immersed in cunning and unfaithfulness, we have decided to forsake it and to escape to where its falseness cannot reach us. We keep house in the wild woods together with our uneducated children. We feed on wild fruit and roots, drink the clear water of springs, and warm ourselves by the light of the sun. Our garment is mossy foliage and grass which serve also as our beds and bedspreads. Our house is a stone cave, from which none will drive out the other. Company and pleasure we find in the wild animals of the woods, for since we do them no harm, they let us live in peace. Thus we live in deserted places and there bring forth our children and grandchildren. . . . [W]e spend our time simply and with humility, awaiting the great change, when in all the world everybody

61 Williams, *Radical Reformation*, pp. 50-57.

will be loyal and pious, and poverty and simplicity will prevail; only then will we leave the forest to dwell among men again.[62]

It is not quite clear to whom Hans Sachs here referred, these pre-Rousseauistic lovers of nature. But in his own age there were many sectarian groups who, combining devotion to the eschatological church (woman) of the wilderness and the venerable monastic impulse to convert the wilderness into an Edenic garden through mutual discipline and obedience to Christ, the Second Adam, fled from the cities into the waste places, for example the Anabaptists in Moravia and the Polish Brethren in Raków. The Dutch Anabaptist Menno Simons (d. 1561) laid the basis for all Mennonite and Amish rural enclaves of Christian peace when he wrote:

He [God] cast out of his mouth the terrible streams of his tyranny, by means of the rulers and the mighty ones of the earth, at the glorious woman pregnant with the Word of the Lord, in hope of exterminating and destroying her seed. But God be eternally praised, who has protected her against the red dragon and has prepared a place in the wilderness for her.[63]

Combining this motif with that of the church as the bride of Christ in the Song of Songs (3:6; 8:5 ff.), as a garden in the wilderness, and the "wilderness church" under Moses in the desert of Sinai, the Pilgrims and Puritans of New England wove powerfully into the conception of the New World the idea that it had been set aside by providence for the reformation of the Reformation and that in the Zion that would emerge millennium and paradise were to be almost as one, as redeemed men learned to live in harmony with the virgin continent.

Passing to the age of science when many scientists still sought to relate their thought and method to scripture and Christian tradition, we note the emergence of the conception of Plastic Nature, an idea that combined the thought of God as the great Artificer and the idea of the *Logos spermatikos*. Over against the radical disjunction made by René Descartes between mind and matter and the relegation of all living creatures except man to the status of soulless and unfeeling machines, were the Cambridge Platonists, notably Ralph Cudworth. An important proponent of what could be called physico-theology, after a representative title of the period,[64] John Ray, in his *The Wisdom of God in the Creation of the World*, called for kindness to animals in express opposition to what seemed the cruel implications of Cartesianism, and he briefly characterized

---

[62] Hans Sachs, *Lament of the Wild Men About the Unfaithful World, Werke*, ed. H. von Keller and E. Goetze (Tübingen, 1870-1908), XXX, pp. 561-564; quoted in Richard Bernheimer, *Wild Men in the Middle Ages* (Cambridge, 1952), p. 114.

[63] "The True Christian Faith," *Complete Writings of Mennon Simons*, ed. by Leonard Verduin (Scottdale, Pa., 1956), pp. 324 f.

[64] Ralph Cudworth, *Physico-Theology: or, a Demonstration of the Being and Attributes of God*, from his *Works of Creation* (London, 1722).

the doctrine of Plastic Nature, ascribing it to Cudworth: "God uses for these effects [the detailed working out of the creative process] the subordinate ministry of some inferior Plastic Nature; as, in his Works of Providence, he doth of Angels."[65]

Cudworth's own description should be quoted because of the long and important career of the idea of plastic nature,[66] but more particularly because it provides a metaphysical basis for especially the English sense of intimacy with nature:

> That every thing in Nature should be done immediately by God himself, this, as according to Vulgar Apprehension, it would render Divine Providence Operose, Sollicitous and Distractious, and thereby make the Belief of it to be entertained with greater difficulty, and give advantage to Atheists. . . . [Plastic Nature] is a certain *Lower Life* than the *Animal*, which acts *Regularly* and *Artifically*, according to the direction of *Mind* and *Understanding, Reason* and *Wisdom*, for *Ends*, or in Order to *Good*, though it self do not know the Reason of what it does, nor is *Master* of that Wisdom according to which it acts, but only a *Servant* to it, and *Drudging Executioner* of the same; it operating *Fatally* and *Sympathetically*, according to *Laws* and *Commands*, prescribed to it by a *Perfect Intellect*, and imprest upon it; and which is either a *Lower* Faculty of some *Conscious Soul*; or else an Inferior kind of Life or *Soul* by self; but essentially depending upon a *Higher Intellect*.[67]

The opposing tradition of nature as malign has been most fully developed in the modern period. In the age of Charles Darwin, Alfred Tennyson recognized over against the earlier Romantics like William Wordsworth with his intimations in nature of immortality that "nature is red in tooth and claw." Matthew Arnold in his poem, which ironically belies the title, "In Harmony with Nature," enjoined:

> Know, man hath all which Nature hath, and more,
> And in that *more* lie all his hopes of good.
> Nature is cruel, man is sick of blood;
> Nature is stubborn, man would fain adore;
>
> Nature is fickle, man hath need of rest;
> Nature forgives no debt, and fears no grave;
> Man would be mild, and with safe conscience blest.
>
> Man must begin, know this, where Nature ends;
> Nature and man can never be fast friends.
> Fool, if thou canst not pass her, rest her slave![68]

---

65 Cudworth, *ibid.*, ed. of 1743, p. 52.

66 William Hunter, "The Seventeenth-Century Doctrine of Plastic Nature, *Harvard Theological Review*, XLIII (1950), p. 213.

67 Ralph Cudworth, *The True Intellectual System of the Universe*, (London, 1678), Ch. III, Sect. xxxvii, Par. 4, 26.

68 Matthew Arnold, "In Harmony with Nature," quoted in Joseph Warren Beach, *The Concept of Nature in Nineteenth-Century English Poetry* (New York, 1936), p. 398.

The American novelist Frank Norris (d. 1902) in his *The Octopus* pictured man as having to cower from a trampling nature:

> Let . . . the insect rebel [man] strive to make head against the power of this nature, and at once it becomes relentless, a gigantic engine, a vast power, huge, terrible; a leviathan with a heart of steel, knowing no compunction, no forgiveness, no tolerance; crushing out the human atom with soundless calm, the agony of destruction sending never a jar, never the faintest tremor through all that prodigious mechanism of wheels and cogs.[69]

The popular science writer and educator Edwin E. Slosson (d. 1929), of whom to be sure, we only postulate a Christian background, expressed the hatred of nature as malign even more harshly:

> Love nature? Never! She is our treacherous and unsleeping foe, ever to be feared and watched and circumvented, for at any moment and in spite of all our vigilance she may wipe out the human race by famine, pestilence, or earthquake and within a few centuries obliterate every trace of its achievement.[70]

In our age of mass wars, genocide, widespread pollution, technological terracide, the global population explosion, and the terror of atomic anihilation, it is hard to know whether it is the human or the creaturely nature that we are to perceive as malign.

(To be concluded in the next issue)

[69] Frank Norris, "The Octopus," *Works*, I, p. 174; quoted in Culmsee, *op. cit.*, p. 29.
[70] Quoted by Carlton F. Culmsee, *op. cit.*, p. 5; source unidentified.

In the following pages George Huntston Williams *of Harvard Divinity School concludes his study entitled, "Christian Attitudes Towards Nature." In the previous issue Professor Williams traced four recurrent antinomies in the Christian understanding of nature. The remaining three antinomies are discussed here.*

Christian Attitudes Toward Nature
CONTINUED

V. THE BOOK OF NATURE AND THE BOOK OF SCRIPTURE: MUTUALLY EXCLUSIVE OR COMPLEMENTARY

Given the formative anti-Canaanite thrust of biblical religion, it was late in the development of the theology of Israel that it became possible for the Jew to look upon the created order as an emblem of the Creator of heaven and earth.[71] The whole of the opposition of prophetic Hebraism to the chthonic cults of fertility, ritual fornication, and sacrifice of the first-born is caught up in the characteristic remonstrances of Jeremiah 2:20 or Isaiah 57:5 against Israel or individual Israelites going a whoring under every green tree. But over against the suspicion of nature and its fecundity there emerge also some of the majestic passages about nature in the same prophets cited and in others. The same Isaiah (55:8) could emphatically establish distance between God and even the elect of Israel, appealing to the cycle of the rains and the seasons: "For my thoughts are not your thoughts, neither are your ways my ways." And Job (38:4) could be asked: "Where were you when I laid the foundations of the earth?"; and elsewhere Job (41:15, 19)could be instructed to look humbly at nature to sense man's being but a part of the whole creation: "Behold Behemoth, [the hippopotmus of the Jordan marshes], which I made as I made you . . . He is the first of the works of God." There is also Proverbs 6:6: "Go to the ant, thou sluggard consider her ways and be wise." But none of these and kindred Old Testament passages go so far as to construe the created order as a supplementary scroll of divine revelation. Nor is this true of the New Testament. But Jesus in his nature parables did lay the basis for a much later Christian development of a theology of nature. For where the Old Testament prophets had at intervals come to ask the believer to behold the created order to see emblems of the Creator, Jesus in

71 Werner Hoffmann, *Israels Stellung zur Natur* (Königsberg, 1928).

36

the parables asked them to consider as well as behold them, a more intensive contemplation being implied, e.g. Matthew 6:26 (Luke 12:24): "Behold/consider the birds of the air/the ravens that they sow not" and v. 28 (27): "Consider the lilies." Jesus' recommendation of a direct reading, as it were, of the book of nature was qualified, however, by St. Paul. It was to be sure, Paul who laid the basis for what later became defined as natural theology in Romans 8, especially v. 19: "Ever since the creation of the world his [God's] invisible nature, namely, his eternal power and deity, has been clearly perceived in the things that have been made. So they [without the book of Scripture] are without excuse." But divergent interpretations of the phrase "without excuse" came to separate a positive and a negative tradition with respect to the practicality and validation of natural theology.

In a broad sense, one major current of Christian thought has held indeed that mankind is without excuse, that reason, even fallen reason, is capable of perceiving at least dimly the traces of God in the created order and these by the means of the faculty of natural reason unillumined by any special revelation. This confidence in the capacity of reason to prove the existence of God through, and to discern his basic laws in, nature came to be dogmatically defined for Roman Catholicism in the constitution *De fide catholica*, chap. 2 of the First Vatican Council in 1870.

The other major current, climaxing in classical Protestantism in the sixteenth century and restated in the Neo-Orthodoxy, among others, of Karl Barth, has taken seriously the context of Paul's acknowledgment of a natural theology, which in chapter 8 in fact so stresses the proneness of fallen reason to perversion that the science of natural theology can remain but theoretical: as it were, the inchoate knowledge of Adam before the fall.

Ranged in the major line of development were most of the ancient Greek Fathers, most of the medieval Schoolmen, much of Anglicanism in the more catholic line, the more rationalist forms of the Radical Reformation, some post-Reformation phases of Calvinism and even Lutheranism, and almost all post-Tridentine Roman Catholicism. Into the line of natural theology fit such works as the *De divisione naturae* of John Scotus Eriugena (d. c. 877), the *Summa contra Gentiles* of Thomas Aquinas (d. 1274), *The Laws of Ecclesiastical Polity* of Richard Hooker (d. 1600), *Christianity not Mysterious* of John Toland (d. 1722), *The Analogy of Religion, Natural and Revealed, to the Constitution and Course of Nature* of Bishop Joseph Butler (d. 1752), *Evidences of Christianity* of William Paley (d. 1805), and *The Ascent of Man* of Henry Drummond (d. 1897). But as massive and as important as is the body of natural theology produced by Christians of diverse confessional jurisdictions over the centuries, their subject matter and approach are not identical with a theology of nature. To be sure, Christian divines, whether in natural theology or in the theology of nature, alike presuppose that all men have access to a certain amount of natural religion as distinct from revealed religion. To be sure, also, Christian divines in many of the works in natural theology have not only striven to rehabilitate reason as a fit instrument for descrying God in his creation, but some of them also, sometimes quite elaborately as did Paley in the *Evidences*, have scrutinized nature in considerable scientific detail. Thus, though natural theology and the theology of nature or creation have in fact creation in common and usually a common recognition of the authority of revealed religion in Scripture, the approaches are somewhat different. In any case, under the contrasting designations of the Book of Nature and the Book of Scripture or their equivalents over the centuries a rather more specialized approach to nature in Christian history is now to be briefly noted. And although a sketch of the phases of natural theology would bring us into contact with the development of science and hence with the main line of the perennial conflict and accommodation between reason and revelation, science and theology, we shall confine ourselves to the subsidiary and more manageable rubric of the two books. When eventually the Book of Nature or the Creatures comes to be contrasted with the Book of Scripture or of Grace, the scriptural references turn out to be: in the Old Testament: Ezekiel 22:10: "And he [God] spread it [the book] before me; and it had writing on the front and on the back," and in the New Testament: Revelation 5:1: "And I saw in the right hand of him who was seated on the throne a scroll written within and on the back." Much would in due course be made of the mysterious book or scroll written both within and without to constitute the scriptural sanction for the developing idea of two revelatory books, of which one was nature.[72]

Before characterizing the theology of nature embodied in the concept of the two books, respectively of emblemic Nature and of verbal Revelation, we must say a word about the related genre of the bestiary. The Christian bestiary was a natural history, which drew upon such classical models as the fabulous in Aesop and the scientific in Pliny, but which besides giving factual and legendary material about the animal kingdom, also assigned moral and even symbolic significance to the creatures and their habits, weaving also scriptural materials into the accounts. For example, in the bestiary the male pelican was interpreted as a paradigm of Christ. The parent pelican had been observed feeding fishes to its young from the pouched beak. As observed and then described in lands where the bird was not directly known, the beaked progeny were thought to be jabbing the bloodied parent to obtain nourishment and causing it to die that they might live off its inner parts.

The oldest bestiary is the *Physiologus* in Greek, parts of which may go back to the second century in Egypt with possibly some Indian sources reflec-

---

[72] The fullest account of the development of the two books is that of Ernst R. Curtius, "The Book of Nature," *European Literature and the Latin Middle Ages*, tr. Willard R. Trask (New York, 1953), pp. 319-26. A standard account of the larger theme is Clement C. J. Webb, *Studies in the History of Natural Theology* (Oxford, 1915).

ting the journey of Alexander the Great to the East. The work was first quoted by the Fathers in the fourth century.[73] The Spanish encyclopedist Bishop Isidore of Seville (d. 636) absorbed and elaborated much in this line in his very influential *Etymologies*.[74] Bestiaries, reaching their allegorical and iconographic apogee in the Latin West in the thirteenth and fourteenth century, continue to the present day, transmuted in popular characterizations of the denizens of the animal world and in children's stories. Without minimizing the tremendous influence on Christian attitudes towards nature of the bestiaries, we take up the theologically more serious permutations of the idea of the two books.

An early reference to the book of nature is in a sermon ascribed to Augustine:

Some people, in order to discover God, read books. But there is a great book: the very appearance of created things. Look above you! Look below you! Note it; read it. God, whom you want to discover, never wrote that book with ink; instead He set before your eyes the things that He had made. Can you ask for a louder voice than that? Why, heaven and earth shout to you: 'God made me!'[75]

The Saxon mystical theologian of Paris, Hugh of St. Victor (d. 1141) in *De sacramentis*[76] combining the hexaemeral and natural theological traditions, with Augustine's conception of the history of the two cities, divided universal history into three epochs, that of the law of nature, that of the written law, and the time of grace. Something from that pre-Mosaic period, he held, lives on into the period of the Christian Church and the grace of Christ applicable to all mankind, the natural law and God's book of creation.[77]

Alan of Lille (1128-1202), as a medieval interpreter of the Book of Nature, in his *The Complaint of Nature* gives us the lines:

> Every creature of the world
> Like unto a book and picture
> To us a mirror is.[78]

The world as macrocosm was for Alan a picture of man, the microcosm, the four elements of the cosmos corresponding to the four humors of the human

[73] It appears in many versions in several languages. The basic Greek text has been critically edited by F. Sbordone (Milan, 1936).

[74] Migne, *PL*, LXXXII.

[75] Angelo Mai, *Nova Bibliotheca Patrum*, I *Augustinus* (Rome, 1852), sermo cxxvi, 6, p. 202. This is quoted in Hugh Pope, *St. Augustine of Hippo* (London, 1937), p. 249, amid a whole chapter, vi, entitled "St. Augustine and the World of Nature," pp. 228-253. It is quite probable, however, that this particular sermon is really not from Augustine.

[76] Translated by R. J. Deferrari (Boston, 1951).

[77] Migne, *PL*, XLXXVI, col. 644 D.

[78] *De planctu naturae; PL*, CCX, col. 579A; *The Complaint of Nature*, Tr. by Douglas M. Moffat, Yale Studies in English, No. 36 (New York, 1908).

constitution. He saw nature as the vicar of God or his handmaiden in the administration of the world and the ministration to man:

> For I, as I work, am not able to press my step in the footprints of God as He works, but I contemplate Him in His activity from a long way off, as it were with longing. His operation is simple, mine is multiform; His work is faultless, mine is defective; His is marvelous, mine is transient; He is incapable of being born, I was born; He is the maker, I am the made; He is the Creator of my work, I am the work of the Creator; He works from nothing; I beg work from another; He works by His own divine will, I work under His name.[79]

In the medieval school of Chartres the whole created order could be looked out upon as a theophany with nature beheld as supplying a cryptic emblem of divinity. The representative encyclopedist of his age, Honorius of Autun (d. c. 1150), in his hexaemeral poem gave winsome expression to this contemplative view.[80] In it Adam and Eve were almost understressed in his poetic rendering of Genesis, the whole created world being given its due. Honorius noted the natural cruelty of the animal world, the predators and the prey, the life cycle, a consequence of the fall of nature. But Honorius held that Christians through grace have been in part already rescued from the worst consequences of the fall, within the disciplines of the Church and urged that kindness to animals be construed as a mark of redemption.

In the order of Francis of Assisi, who gave such an impetus to the kind of outlook we are here attending to, John of Fidanze Bonaventure (d. 1274), biographer of the founder, major theologian, and minister general of the order, made use of the idea of the two books, among other places, in his brief treatise on theology, influential because so compact and persuasive, the *Breviloquium*. This is not in itself a treatise in the theology of nature. It begins with the revealed doctrine of the Trinity. But in the second book on the creation he says: "[W] e gather that the creation of the world is a kind of book."[81] Because of man's fallen condition, however, Bonaventure was convinced that the "double book" which is written on the outside and on the in (Ezekiel 2:9 and Revelation 5:1) can in the end be read only by one in two natures, namely, by Christ *and* by those instructed by him.[82] Thus in Bonaventure the Book of Nature or Creation becomes bound into the Book of Scripture, although in other Franciscans and many others it can emerge as autonomous and complementary to Scripture.

The Belgian Dominican encyclopedist Thomas of Cantimpré (d. c. 1272), absorbing much of the tradition of the bestiary and the tradition of the theology or book of nature, in his *De rerum natura*, laid the basis for much of later

---

[79] Quotes by Glacken, *op. cit.*, p. 218.

[80] Honorius Augustodunensis, *Hexaemeron*, Migne, *PL*, CLXXII, coll. 253-270.

[81] *Breviloquium*, ii, 12, 1; translation of Erwin Esser Nemmers (London, 1946), p. 75.

[82] *Ibid.*, p. 73.

medieval natural theology and the theology of nature and natural history. His book circulated in longer and shorter recension and in several vernacular versions. The German Dominican Conrad of Megenburg (d. 1374) made it available in German as the very influential *Buch der Natur.*

Thomas à Kempis, or whoever, in *De Imitatione Christi* made use of the book of nature theme, subsumed by the book of Christ, when he wrote: "If thy heart be right, then every creature would be a mirror of life and a book of sacred doctrine."[83]

An especially influential late medieval development of the metaphor of the Book of Nature is that of the Catalan Franciscan Raymond Sabundus (d. 1436), whose *Natural Theology* construed the Book of Nature as slightly superior to the Book of Scripture.[84]

The work when translated by Michel de Montaigne (d. 1592) was given wide circulation in France, but so humanized that Nature thereafter would tend in France to mean human nature.[85] In Spain Sabundus lived on in another version of the theology of nature, in the *Simbolo de la fé* of Luis de Granada (d. 1488). In the Netherlands Raymond's two books reappear in the *Confessio Belgica* (1561), article ii, composed largely by Guy de Brès:

We know him [God] by two means: first, by the creation, preservation, and government of the universe; which is before our eyes as a most elegant book, wherein all things existing, great and small, are as so many letters . . . : secondly, . . . by his holy and divine Word.[85a]

Among some Radical Reformers in the sixteenth century the two books were turned into two Gospels. Thought concerning the Books of Nature and Scripture was recast in the contrasting terms of the Gospel *of* all creation (natural theology, which in this sectarian context meant the disclosure of the perennial suffering of the creaturely condition) and the Gospel *to* all creatures. By this phrase was meant that human beings were saved in the recognition that even the Son of God had to bear suffering. The Gospel of all Creation (*aller Kreatur*) was based upon a vernacular rendering of the Dominical injunction in Mark 16:15, but with the original dative converted into a genitive. Suffering in the world, the suffering of all flesh, must be perceived, according to Paracelsus,

[83] *Imitatio Christi*, ii, 4.

[84] Raimundus Sabundus, rector of the University of Toulouse, *Theologia Naturalis seu Liber Creaturarum*, finished in MS 1436; first printed in Lyons 1484; critical edition by Friedrich Stegemuller (Stuttgart, 1966).

[85] *Oeuvres completes*, I, *La Théologie Naturelle de Raymond Sebon* (Paris, 1932).

[85a] The French text with English translation of the Dutch Reformed Confession is printed by Philip Schaff, *The Creeds of Christendom*, 3 vols. (New York, 1878), III, p. 384. On Guy de Brès quite possible direct use of Sabundus, see Johannes Lindeboom, "Art. II der Nederlandse Geloofsbelijdenis en zijn historische achtergrond," W. J. Kooiman and J. M. van Veen, eds., *Pro Regno: Pro Sanctuarios: Een bundel studies . . . bij de zestigste verjaardag van Prof. Dr. G. van der Leeuw* (Nijkerk, 1950), pp. 309-16.

Thomas Müntzer, Hans Hut, Pilgrim Marpeck, and many another before the redemptive suffering of Christ can be fully understood or appropriated.[86]

We may bring our brief sketch of the two-book theme near to a close with a vivid expression of it from the English seventeenth century. In his *Religio Medici* Sir Thomas Browne (d. 1682) wrote:

> Thus there are two Books from whence I collect my Divinity; besides that written one of God, another of His servant Nature, that universal and publick Manuscript that lies expans'd unto the eyes of all, those that never saw him in the one, have discovered him in the other: This was the [sole] Scripture and the Theology of the Heathens. . . . [S]urely the Heathens knew better how to joyne and reade these mysticall letters, than wee Christians, who cast a more caresse eye on these common Hieroglyphicks, and disdain to suck Divinity from the flowers of nature. Nor do I so forget God, as to adore the name of Nature. . . . I hold there is a generall beauty in the works of God, and therefore no deformity in any kind or species of creature whatsoever: I cannot tell by what Logick we [presume to] call a Toad, a Beare, or an Elephant, ugley, they being created in those outward shapes and figures which best expresse the actions of their outward formes. . . . To speake yet more narrowly, there was never any thing ugly, or misshapen, but the Chaos; wherein notwithstanding, to speake strictly, there was no deformity, because no forme, nor was it yet impregnate by the voyce of God: Now nature is not at variance with art, nor art with nature; they both being the servants of his providence: Art is the perfection of Nature: Were the world now as it was the sixt day, there were yet a Chaos; Nature hath made one world, and Art another. In briefe, all things are artificiall, for nature is the Art of God.[87]

Characteristic of the two-book theology is that nature without human beings or their history or even without the direct revelation to the elect among them is capable of communicating a message as from a manuscript. We may in conclusion to this sketch jump two centuries ahead and to America to find a familiar echo of this venerable theology of nature in Christian lands.

Ralph Waldo Emerson, a minister in Boston before he became essayist in Concord and popular lecturer throughout the country and in England, in his essay, *English Traits* (1856), observed: " 'Tis said that the views of nature held by any people determine all their institutions."[88] In this particular context Emerson had primarily in mind human nature, but he, the friend of David Thoreau, would also have made the statement with respect to a society's view of nature at large. Emerson gave us his own idea of nature near the conclusion to the famous essay on *Nature* (1836):

> The world proceeds from the same spirit as the body of man. It is a remoter and inferior incarnation of God, a projection of God in the unconscious. But it differs from the body in one important respect. It is not, like that, now subjected to the human will. Its

---

[86] See further George H. Williams, *The Radical Reformation* (Philadelphia, 1962), esp. pp. 171, 836 f.

[87] *Religio Medici*, Part II, sect. 16; *The Prose of Sir Thomas Browne*, ed. by Norman Endicott (New York/London, 1968), pp. 21f.

[88] Ralph Waldo Emerson, "English Traits," *Works* (Boston, 1885), V, p. 52, critical edition by Merton M. Sealts, Jr. and Alfred R. Ferguson, *Emerson's Nature—Origin, Growth, Meaning* (New York/Toronto, 1969), p. 31.

serene order is inviolable by us. It is, therefore, to us, the present expositor of the divine mind. It is a fixed point whereby we may measure our departure. As we degenerate, ... the contrast between us and our house is more evident. We are as much strangers in nature as we are aliens from God. We do not understand the notes of birds. The fox and the deer run away from us; the bear and tiger rend us. We do not know the uses of more than a few plants [as corn and the apple, the potato and the vine]. Is not the landscape, every glimpse of which hath a grandeur, a face of Him? Yet this may show us what discord is between man and nature, for you cannot freely admire a noble landscape if laborers are digging in the field hard by. The poet finds something ridiculous in his delight until he is out of the sight of men.[89]

Emerson, heir of a long and complex tradition, regarded nature as "the expositor of the divine mind" but only when the observer of the book of nature is removed from his fellowmen or fellow laborers, and even then he remains at once stranger to nature and alien to God, despite the acknowledged fact that the world or nature and the body of man proceed from the same spirit.

We have thus gone back and forth through almost two thousand years of Christian history to catch at intervals one or another of seven strands being woven into the tapestry of Western civilization. For the five themes thus far dealt with, though we have but sampled a few representative periods or persons to make each rubric clear, we have been able to assemble enough material at least to suggest a pattern of thought and to point to its development and permutation among the intertwining themes.

With, however, the two remaining of the seven sets of antinomies, we must be much briefer: with respect to the ensuing theme, the sixth set, because it so readily broadens into the history of politics and culture as a whole; the last of the seven because, though essential to our systematic explanation of seven scriptural motifs, it is actually very sparely represented in Church history.

VI. THE CITY OR THE CULTIVATED (MIDDLE) LANDSCAPE AS THE MEAN BETWEEN THE WICKED CITY AND THE HOWLING WILDERNESS IS THE REALM OF GRACE AND REDEMPTION: THE CONFLICT BETWEEN THE POLITICAL AND PASTORAL METAPHORS

The citation of a great American interpreter of nature, Emerson, who broke with the church and set a pattern for many nature lovers ever since, who would rather spend Sunday in the woods than at formal worship in church, brings us to our sixth set of opposites. We are led from the Book of Nature and the Book of Scripture back to the Book of Scripture alone which, often, however, becomes solely the Book of Man and his kingdoms and polities apart from environing nature, and the recurrent despair of man with his city and its corruptions and his residual fear of wilderness as well.

[89] *Ibid.*, I, pp. 68f.

The sixth set of scriptural opposites is thus as follows: The small town with gardens in the sense of the pastoral or middle landscape with its village, rural, or suburban polity is the mean between the wicked city and the howling wilderness; it is the realm of rural classical, scriptural virtues, of nature shaped by the toil of man but still amply displaying the plenitude of God's creation. *Sed contra:* The Church is preeminently the city or kingdom of God more or less segregated from nature. Salvation occurs in history, not in nature; in political rather than pastoral imagery.

On the garden side are the two preeminent Old Testament texts, relating respectively to the dawn and the destiny of the race. In Genesis 2:15 "The Lord God took the man and put him in the Garden of Eden to till it and keep it;" while the Prophet Isaiah (40:4) foresaw a time when "Every valley will be exalted and every mountain and hill shall be made low" thus bringing back the original contours of the peaceful garden before the fall.

The texts which couch redemption in the political metaphors of Kingdom, City, or Elect People, Holy Nation are, of course, innumerable; but there is one among them which expressly and wholly (of course allegorically) displaces nature in the eschatological City: Rev. 21:1 f.; 23: "Then I saw a new heaven and a new earth; for the first heaven and the first earth had passed away and the sea was no more. And I saw the holy city, new Jerusalem, coming down out of heaven from God, prepared as a bride adorned for her husband. . . . And the city has no need of sun or moon to shine upon it, for the glory of God is its light." The Seer here echoed the prophecy of Isaiah (60:1-3, 17) that "the sun shall be no more thy light."

Although the texts cited are scriptural in line with our overall presentation of the ongoing effects of scriptural passages in the permutations of Christian attitudes towards nature, it should be acknowledged that on the pastoral side the classical tradition bulks very large. While the politicization of salvation and hominization of the world draws very much from the political metaphors of Scripture, the pastoral ideal of the middle landscape between the wicked city and the noisome or fearful wilderness comes very much more out of the classical tributary of Christian civilization.[90] The recent studies of the conflict between city and wilderness in the intellectual history of American have been particularly numerous and insightful. In America the age-old conflict between the city and the countryside, between empire and desert, between the Christianity of burghers and patricians and the Christianity of the gentry and the peasants has

[90] On the pastoral motif and similar material in classical antiquity, see Eugène Secretan, *Du Sentiment de la Nature dans L'Antiquité* (Lausanne, 1866); Katharine Allen, *The Treatment of Nature in the Poetry of the Roman Republic,* (Madison, Wisconsin, 1899); Archibald Geikie, *The Love of Nature among the Romans* (London, 1912); Henry R. Fairclough, *Love of Nature among the Greeks and Romans* (New York, 1930); W. Leonard Grant, *Neo-Latin Literature and the Pastoral* (Chapel Hill, 1965); George Soutar, *Nature in Greek Poetry* (London, 1939); Paul Van Tieghem, *Le sentiment de la Nature dans le Préromantisme Européen* (Paris, 1960).

been recast in terms of town and plantation, with many a modest farmhouse with its classical doorways pointing back to the Jeffersonian-Vergilian ideal of the gentleman farmer amid the middle landscape between the wild mountains and the wicked cities.[91] The American gentleman farmer amid the well cultivated fields and rich pastures and orchards surveys his husbandry as a New Adam uncorrupted by the Old World.

The Quaker primitivist Edward Hicks (d. 1849), in his hundreds of paintings of the Peaceable Kingdom, adapted the metaphor of royal power to describe redeemed man's harmonious control over the disparate and destructive life energies. In barnyard and Edenic scenes he pictured the spiritual man who as husbandman or steward judging all things, domestic and wild animals, and who with Christ within is judged by none.

To trace, however, even in the New World the tension between urban and agrarian Christianity and the concurrent attitudes towards nature presupposed and engendered is altogether too complex for the present conspectus. The sketch would take us into political, economic, cultural, and even horticultural history without directly contributing to the theme being surveyed. We can but mention representative phrases in which salvation in America has been cast in urban and other political metaphors: the Puritan Zion, Nature's nation, Redeemer Nation, the almost chosen people, manifest destiny, the Social Gospel, the Secular City.

Such American Protestant theologians of culture as Harvey Cox and Herbert Richardson fit in here, as anthropocentric urban "exclusionists" in contrast to the often less expressly Christian or even anti-Christian "biocentric inclusivists."[92] Richardson with optimism in "sociotechnics" looks forward to "the creation of a wholly artificial environment."[93] Cox, rejoicing in the emergence of "one immense city," writes: "The world is becoming one huge interdependent city, in which jungles and deserts remain only with the explicit consent of a global metropolis."[94] Even Teihard de Chardin with his evolutionary hominization of

---

[91] Morton and Lucia White have traced the disdain and even fear of the city in American history in *The Intellectual versus the City* (Cambridge, 1962). For the larger account our theme is touched upon more in the title than in the content by Thomas M. Gannon and George W. Traub, *The Desert and the City* (London, 1969). Other works on the conflict in America particularly are Henry Nash Smith *Virgin Land* (Cambridge, 1950); Hans Huth, *Nature and the American* (Berkeley, 1957); Charles L. Sanford, *The Quest for Paradise* (Urbana, Ill., 1961); Arthur A. Ekirch, Jr, *Man and Nature in America* (New York, 1963); Leo Marx, *The Machine in the Garden* (New York, 1964); Roderick Nash, *Wilderness and the American Mind* (New Haven, 1967); Paul Shepard, *Man in the Landscape* (New York, 1967); Frank Gibson, *Man's Dominion: The Story of Conservation in America* (New York, 1971); Frank Darling, *Wilderness and Plenty* (New York, 1971); Eric Rust, *Nature: Garden or Desert?* (Waco, Texas, 1971).

[92] See the critique of Elder, *op. cit.*, ch. iv.

[93] *Toward an American Theology* (New York, 1967), p. 17. Noted by Elder, *op. cit.*, p. 69.

[94] *On Not Leaving It to the Snake* (New York, 1967), p. 102; noted by Elder, *op. cit.*, p. 73.

the biosphere tends to exlude the other species from fulfilment in the noosphere. Even in Pope Paul something of the hominization of the outer spheres was implied when he chose, in a gesture of solidarity and goodwill, to write out Psalm 8 to be carried by the first Astronuauts to land on the moon: "When I look . . . at the moon . . . which thou hast established, what is man that thou art mindful of him? . . . Thou hast given him dominion over the works of thy hands; thou hast put all things under his feet." The Pope afterwards spoke of the Astronauts as "conquering the moon"; and perhaps thereby unwittingly he sanctioned the absorption of even the second great luminary of creation into the Secular City of Man, as once his papal predecessor divided the newly discovered Western hemisphere between the Portuguese and the Spanish conquistadores. Our allusion to the great Jesuit paleontologist Teihard brings us from the middle landscape between wilderness and city and the conflict between the pastoral and the urban metaphor to our final set of contrasts.

VII. MANKIND ONLY OR THE WHOLE CREATION
SUBJECT TO SALVATION

The seventh set of opposites is as follows: Human beings are alone the objects of salvation. *Sed contra:* All nature or all creation is to be conserved, fulfilled, redeemed. The Old Testament *locus classicus* for the more comprehensive view of salvation is no doubt hyperbolic Isaiah 11:6: "The wolf shall dwell with the lamb, and the leopard shall lie down with the kid, and the calf and the lion and the fatling together, and a little child shall lead them." Akin to it in the language of the covenant is the prophecy in Hosea 2:18 expressly over against the nature worship as directed to the *baalim:* "And I will make for you on that day a covenant with the beasts of the field, the birds of the air, and the creeping things of the ground; and I will abolish the bow, the sword, and war from the land. . . ." Two New Testament *loci* are commonly referred to as sanction for the restoration or consummation of all things, *apokatastasis pantōn.* They are Acts 3:21: "Whom the heaven must receive until the times of restitution of all things, which God hath spoken by the mouth of all his holy prophets since the world began,"[95] and, I Corinthians 15:28: "And when all things shall be subdued unto him, then shall the Son also himself be subject unto him that put all things under him, that God may be all in all."

That human beings are the object of salvation, or at least the faithful or the elect or those within the Church, outside of which there may well be no salvation, is of course not in need of development here. Of some interest, however, is the place of nature beyond man in the Christian schemes of salvation. This eschatological aspect of the understanding of nature is thus the

---

95 The Dominical word in Mark 9:12 that "Elijah comes first to restore all things" does not have a cosmic sense.

fitting conclusion of the series of seven sets of scriptural tests and the eschatological counterpart of the first set. It will be recalled that the first set dealt with the question of whether man implicated the rest of nature in the fall, corrupting it; and related to that but still distinct was the second set as to whether, despite the fall or because of the fall, human nature or nature in general is getting worse, remains constant, or under tutelage is improving in preparation for God's direct rule.

Origen, whom we recall earlier in this paper as having been thoroughly anthropocentric about creation, was eventually condemned by the Church for his universalism based in part upon the foregoing scriptural passages but also for drawing from ambient classical sources. It is true that he thought of the eventual restoration of all things in terms primarily human and angelic. He trusted that the fallen angels, that is the devil and the demons, would all be saved. He included in salvation also the stars, for like many of the classical writers and the Church Fathers he held that the perfect spheres had souls. In the course of Christian history and, perhaps one should say also heretical Christian history, universalism or the doctrine of the ultimate salvation of all things recurs in many overt and covert forms. The development has never been thoroughly researched. It is intimately related to the development of the feeling of kindness and concern for the creaturely kingdom, which this writer wishes he had had time to pursue *pari passu* with the Christian attitude toward nature in general, for the harmony of man with the beasts in Paradise and the concern of Noah to save more than merely the clean, that is, the usable animals, have slowly exercised a moderating influence on monk, friar, and finally the lay Christian in his dealings with animals.[96] But we push ahead to the sixteenth century to single out a most explicit proponent of the salvation of the animal kingdom.

In John Bradford, royal chaplain under Edward and martyr at the fiery stake under Mary in 1555, we observe an extraordinary concern for the redemption of the realm of the creatures. Bradford in his meditation on "Thy kingdom come" in the Lord's Prayer distinguished betwen God's present kingship over all creatures in general like the demons, the angels, mankind everywhere, the animals, the birds, the fishes, and all other creatures, and his imminent personal rule over the elect. The elect pilgrimage through the wilderness of the world and Bradford thanks God that he "maketh this world unto us a wilderness." But he looked forward to the absorption of the greater kingdom in the lesser, that all might be saved.

Just before his execution, in the *Restoration of All Things*, dependent in part on Martin Bucer, Bradford clearly propounded a doctrine of a truly

---

[96] We may, however, cite some of the secondary literature: John Oswald, *The Cry of Nature, or, an Appeal to Mercy and to Justice, on behalf of the Persecuted Animals* (London, 1791); Edward Byron Nicholson, *The Rights of an Animal: A New Essay in Ethics* (London, 1879); and Roswell C. McRea, *The Humane Movement* (New York, 1910).

universal salvation or restitution of all things, interpreting the term *creature* in its fullest sense. Appealing to Paul's outcry for the whole of creation groaning in pain together with man because of the Fall (Romans 8:22), and alluding to the angels (and the peaceable animals) serving Christ in the wilderness of temptation, Bradford proclaimed that "without any doubt" all creatures, that is, "plants, beasts, and other living things," would be freed along with men and restored to the perfection and harmony of Paradise.[97]

In seventeenth-century England, the leveler and moralist Richard Overton declared in reference to the *apokatastasis* of Acts 3:21:

... the *Gospel* or *Glad Tydings* is unto all, all are under hope, and all things, *men, beasts, and birds* shall be made new, or restored at the Resurrection, and so *Death shall be swallowed up in victory.* ....[98]

William Bowling of Cranbrock, Kent, a dissenter of uncertain affiliation, declared: "That Christ shed his bloud for kine and horses and all creatures, as well as for men. . . ."[99]

Without this specificity and individuality the already mentioned Bishop Goodman of Gloucester in his *Religion of Dumbe Creatures* (1622) declared:

For certain it is of all the dumbe creatures, that at the generall day of our Resurrection, they likewise, though not in themselves, yet in their own elements and principles, shall be renewed. For there shall be a new heaven and a new earth ... that may be fitted for our use."[100]

The narrow strand of expectation that even the non-human creaturely world might be included in the redemptive restoration of all things survived into the nineteenth century and in an unusual spokesman for the view. The Unitarian clerical chemist, Joseph Priestley (d. 1804), friend and correspondent of Thomas Jefferson, once reflected on the possibility that animals might be resurrected to share in the life of bliss: "[T]he great misery, to which some of them are exposed in their life, may incline us to think that a merciful and just God will make them some recompense for it hereafter. He is *their* Maker and Father as well as *ours.*"[101]

---

[97] John Bradford, "The Restoration of All Things," *Writings,* ed. Aubrey Townsend (London, 1853), II, p. 127; I, pp. 351-364. See further: D. P. Walker, *The Decline of Hell* (Chicago, 1964), pp. 67, 73f; C. A. Patrides, "The Salvation of Satan," *Journal of the History of Ideas,* XXVIII (1967), 467-78.

[98] *Mans Mortalitie* (London, 1644); ed. by Harold Fisch, English Reprints Series, No. 21 (Liverpool, 1968); p. 70.

[99] Preserved in Thomas Edwards, *Gangraena,* 2nd ed. (London, 1646), III, pp. 36 f, Item 5.

[100] Goodman, Praysing, pp. 28f.; quoted by Soden, *op. cit.,* p. 124.

[101] Joseph Priestely, "Disquisitions Relating to Matter and Spirit," *Works,* III (1777), p. 383.

CONCLUSION

We have sampled, almost at random through the centuries, divergent ways in which Christians, informed by Scripture and looking out upon creation, considered (i) whether all creatures had been implicated in the fall of Adam; (ii) whether, if independent of human sinfulness, the creaturely world were running down or remaining constant (or even advancing), (iii) whether nature might independently of man praise God in harmony and functional joy or could only be of meaning as subsumed under man either as (a) steward of as (b) exploiter; (iv) whether nature, including the virgin wilderness, were benign or indifferent or hostile to man; (v) whether nature were a complementary revelation of the divine; (vi) whether the realm of grace and salvation were better cast in political or pastoral metaphors; and (vii) whether nature itself or only man can be subject to redemption.

In our very critical situation, Christians must set themselves the task of reassessing the richness of this complex scriptural heritage and attempt, as long ago with such doctrines as Triadology and Christology, to draw out in our age the fuller implications of our creedal formula "Creator of heaven and earth" and so to amplify the doctrine of creation and so to elaborate therefrom an earth ethic that we shall be enabled to reshape our lives and institutions and installations for dwelling more harmoniously on what has emerged, in the astronautical vision of our time, as at once our earthly and our heavenly home.

At the Fourth Ecumenical Council of Chalcedon in 451 the Church Fathers, having long toiled theologically and indeed quarreled bitterly over the seemingly disparate texts testifying both to the divinity and the humanity of Jesus Christ, came to the dogmatic definition of him as one Person in two natures. In some such way there remains for theologians today and tomorrow the ongoing task of perfecting the Christian doctrine of man and the virtually untouched task of formulating a Christian doctrine of creation. And at the end of the process, which will surely involve the plenary assimilation of the data of the natural and the social sciences, we shall be in a better position to understand human being, human existence, as also the impersonation of two natures. Surely one of the natures of man is continuous with the created order. But he also believes that he has been created in the image of God (Genesis 1:27), though from the dust of the earth (2:7). Christian anthropology must further explore, clarify, and interrelate the juncture in human personhood of the seeming antinomies in the scriptural texts concerning creation at large and man in nature.

Are we in the end conquerors of the cosmos or carers for our fellow creatures, stewards of creation or exploiters, ruthless like some of the beasts or redemptive of them all and therewith mankind, manipulative or reverent toward life in all its mysterious plenitude; are we a benignant or a malign species, crowding ourselves and reducing the myriad forms of life, pessimistic or optimistic about nature and our human nature evolved from it, a people at home in the secular city or in the countryside and the open spaces or belonging to and improving the quality of both? These are deep questions raised in our tradition and deserving of reexamination in the present environmental and moral crisis.

What prompted the writer as minister, Church historian, and conservationist to consider such a study was an interest in the conservation both of wildlife and of natural resources for the generations and for the societies not yet evolved and the concern to help restrain society's ruthless onslought upon the created order and the pollution and spoilation of the general environment and the destruction of wildlife. In our not quite random soundings of Church history we have found that the richness and the variety of Christian and secularized Christian attitudes could be provisionally put into some kind of order under seven recurrent sets of seeming antinomies, which have yielded altogether more than a dozen recurrent modes of thought in Christian history. Cumulatively the first or the second thrust in each of these seven sets amount to a major and a minor tradition with respect to redeemed man's attitude toward nature. Thus far the major thrust involving domination and exclusion of nature from man's stewardly concern has prevailed and been indeed a component in the evolution of our technological civilization. But the minor strand, like the dissenting opinion in constitutional law, has been brought out in every epoch to be restated in our own age, when there must be a new stress upon the creaturely world, no doubt for man's own well being but also for the sake of the wild world itself.

Christians, with their sense for nature as a creation which implies the Creator, are strategically located with their ministries, properties, educational programs, and publications to be especially effective in calling upon the rich and half-forgotten elements in our tradition and in bringing them to bear upon the current scene.

Hindus and Buddhists notably among the world religionists and many Christians as well have argued that the Judaeo-Christian tradition, which has shaped Western civilization, has been essentially hostile to nature and is therefore ultimately responsible for the bulldozer mentality which is now associated with technocratic societies. But surely the thrust of all the passages adduced from the history of Christianity would point to unexpected resources for a reevaluation of both human nature and nature in general. In brief may it be given to us severally and collectively, by safeguarding something of the real wilderness left in the world, to reclaim the wilderness of man within and to convert the urban wasteland and the rural slum into a garden, fit for both disciplined human beings and wild beasts.

Church people in general and perhaps ministers in particular can become qualified environmentalists in the extension of their ministry from ghetto to globe. Who more than ministers, proclaiming the faith of the communion of saints, a community in time and space, a community that includes the past and also the as yet unborn generations, could better mount the watchtowers and sound the alert for the care of the earth?

Related GHW Bibliography

"Wilderness and Paradise in the History of the Church," *Church History* 28 (1959), 3-24.

"The Seminary in the Wilderness: A Representative Episode in the Cultural History of Northern New England," *Harvard Library Bulletin* 13 (1959), 27-58.

Wilderness and Paradise in Christian Thought: The Biblical Experience of the Desert in the History of Christianity and the Paradise Theme in the Theological Idea of the University (New York: Harper & Brothers, 1962).

"Christian Attitudes Toward Nature," *Christian Scholar's Review* 2 (1971-72), 3-35, 112-126. Expansion of article in *Colloquy* 3 (1970), 12-15.

"Ecology and Abortion," *New England Sierran* 3, 6 (1972), 2, 6.

"Creatures of a Creator, Members of a Body, Subjects of a Kingdom," *To God be the Glory: Sermons in Honor of George Arthur Buttrick*, ed. Theodore Gill (Nashville: Abingdon, 1973), 98-108.

"The Idea of the Wilderness of the New World in Cotton Mather's *Magnalia Christi Americana*," *Magnalia Christi Americana* I, eds. Kenneth Murdock and Elizabeth Miller (Cambridge: Harvard UP, 1977), 49-58.

GHW Festschrifts

Continuity and Discontinuity in Church History: Essays Presented to George Huntston Williams on the Occasion of His 65th Birthday, ed. F. Forrester Church and Timothy George (Leiden: Brill, 1979).

The Contentious Triangle: Church, State and University. A Festschrift in Honor of Professor George Huntston Williams, ed. Rodney L. Peterson and Calvin Augustine Pater (Kirksville, MO: Truman State University Press, 1999).

Selective Ecotheology Bibliography

Berry, R. J., ed. *Environmental Stewardship: Critical Perspectives–Past and Present*. (London: T. & T. Clark, 2006).

Berry, Thomas. *The Dream of the Earth*. (San Francisco: Sierra Club Books, 1988)

Berry, Wendell. *The Art of the Commonplace: The Agrarian Essays of Wendell Berry*. Ed. Norman Wirzba. (Berkeley, CA: Counterpoint, 2002).

Bouma-Prediger, Steven. *For the Beauty of the Earth: A Christian Vision for Creation Care, 2d. ed.* (Grand Rapids: Baker, 2010).

Daniel Brunner, et al *Introducing Evangelical Ecotheology*.(Grand Rapids: Baker, 2014).

Carson, Rachel. 1962. *Silent Spring*. (Boston: Houghton Mifflin, 1962).

DeWitt, Calvin B. *Caring for Creation: Responsible Stewardship of God's Handiwork.* (Grand Rapids: Baker, 1998).

Houghton, John. *Global Warming: the Complete Briefing,* 4th ed. (Cambridge: Cambridge University Press, 2009).

McKibbon, Bill. *The End of Nature.* 2d ed. (New York: Random House, 2006)

Rasmussen, Larry. *Earth Honoring Faith: Religious Ethics in a New Key* (New York: Oxford UP, 2012).

Santmire, H. Paul. *The Travail of Nature: The Ambiguous Ecological Promise of Christian Theology.* (Philadelphia: Fortress Press, 1985).

Sittler, Joseph. *Evocations of Grace: The Writings of Joseph Sittler on Ecology, Theology, and Ethics.* Ed. Steven Bouma-Prediger & Peter Bakken (Grand Rapids: Eerdmans, 2000).

White, Lynn. "The historical roots of our ecologic crisis." *Science* 155, no. 3767 (10 March, 1967): 1203-7.

Wilkinson, Katherine. *Between God and Green* (New York: Oxford UP, 2012).

www.ingramcontent.com/pod-product-compliance
Lightning Source LLC
Chambersburg PA
CBHW061754040426
42447CB00011B/2299